Gods Behaving Badly

Gods Behaving Badly

Media, Religion, and Celebrity Culture

Pete Ward

BAYLOR UNIVERSITY PRESS

Cover Design by Nicole Weaver, Zeal Design Studio
Cover image © iStockphoto.com/Forrest Brown

Ward, Pete, 1959-
  Gods behaving badly : media, religion, and celebrity culture /
Pete Ward.
       p. cm.
  Includes bibliographical references and index.
  ISBN 978-1-60258-150-0 (pbk. : alk. paper)
  1. Popular culture--Religious aspects. 2. Celebrities. I. Title.
  BL65.C8W366 2011
  201'.7--dc22
                                    2010020209

Printed in the United States of America on acid-free paper with a
minimum of 30% pcw recycled content.

CONTENTS

INTRODUCTION

Media and popular culture make up one of the fastest-growing areas
in the study of religion. An entire range of studies focuses on religion
and how it is portrayed, and changed, by the media. These include work
examining religion and film, religion and advertising, religion and TV,
and religion and popular music.[1] Individual TV shows, rock bands, and
movies have been mined for their "theology," and the lived experiences
of fans have been explored to see how and to what extent they construct
religious meaning from popular culture. What all of this work has in
common is the sense that the boundaries between popular culture and
religion are blurring. As we begin to see the extent to which popular culture operates in religious ways and carries religious meanings, there is a
growing perception that previous distinctions between the religious and
the secular, the sacred and the profane, are collapsing into one another.
The investigation of celebrity culture forms a part of this ongoing project on the changing nature of religion in popular culture.

Celebrity is ubiquitous; it has come to dominate media discourses
in every field of life, from sports and politics to the arts and the environment. Celebrity-focused gossip magazines and Web sites have mush-
roomed, serious newspapers now have celebrity columns, and soap opera
plots are given front-page headlines in the tabloid press. Celebrity is not

simply an aspect of popular culture—celebrity is part of popular culture's DNA. Even if we have very little interest in celebrities, we seem to know about them. In fact, we don't just know about celebrities—we may well have somehow formed opinions about them. A great deal of celebrity gossip will pass us by, but we might still have a view to share about Bono, Britney, Demi, Michael, or Brad. Celebrity culture tempts us off the sidelines. It actively invites us to form a view and make a judgment. Some might say that celebrity culture is a kind of virus infecting all cultural life. Yet irritation with the pointlessness of celebrities is in many ways a key element in celebrity culture.

On Celebrity Religion: A Word to Its Cultured Despisers

The chattering classes like to affect an indifference to celebrity. They do not watch reality TV, and they would never buy a gossip rag. Most are agreed that the whole celebrity thing is froth, ephemeral, the antithesis of all things of value. In the main, this approach to celebrity is a thinly veiled version of an elitist view of culture. The religious version of this merges taste with some kind of ecclesial preference. Here celebrity culture is seen as representing the spiritual collapse of contemporary society, proof that for the large part we are living in an empty and vacuous society.

The renewed interest in religion and popular culture has gone a long way toward redressing some of these assumptions. Yet while academics in the field of religion and theology have started to work with some elements of popular culture, celebrity can still trigger some version of the elitist view of popular culture. As I have hinted, actually this is part of the game. Celebrity culture thrives on the fact that we take a view and we form a judgment. It wants us to take the moral high ground. From the *National Enquirer* and *Heat* magazine to the *New York Times* and the *Guardian* newspapers, the subplot of celebrity discourse is (im)morality. So it doesn't really matter if the question posed is who looks the best on the catwalk, or if the celebrity model is overweight or underweight, or whether this star should be allowed to adopt a child from the developing world, or if our appreciation for a pop star's music should be influenced by their conviction for a sex crime—at root we are being drawn into a conversation about what we do and do not value.

Celebrities are significant not because they have any inherent skills, talents, genius, or even achievements. Most celebrities seem not to have achieved very much, and they can often be rather talentless. Celebrities matter not because of who they are but because of what they represent. It is the meanings that become attached to celebrities as they appear in the media that form their currency in the circulation of popular culture. Celebrities, in other words, are a part of the signifying system of popular culture. They function as symbols in the flow of communication. As such, celebrities offer a myriad of different "takes" on what is possible in consumer culture, representing different ways to be a woman, to be black, to be old, to be faithful, to be gay, to be a parent, to be unfaithful, to be a loser, to fail. In fact, they mediate a range of possible ways of being human.

Our interest in celebrities, or indeed our lack of interest in them, is rooted in the extent to which we relate to what they represent. We may identify with them or we may disidentify with them. So as we casually flick through a magazine, glancing at the pictures, we are being invited into decisions about our possible selves. The question that we might ask when trying on a new piece of clothing—"Is this me?"—is essentially what is going on as we engage with celebrities in their various media incarnations. In this context the dismissal of celebrity culture by intellectuals and religious people is a genuine response. They are saying, "I don't like that," or "I'm not interested in that. It is not me." The quality press accommodates these views partly by printing mildly condemnatory articles about the excesses of celebrity culture and partly by fostering an interest in personalities in the arts, sports, and politics. This strategy, however, is not separate from celebrity culture; in fact, it is part of it while it pretends to rise above it.

CELEBRITY WORSHIP

For commentators and critics, the close identification that many people seem to have with celebrities is suggestive of a religious analogy. Celebrities are routinely called idols, or icons, and from time to time they are called "divine" or even referred to as "gods." Fans are said to be devoted to celebrities, to adore them, and in many cases the behavior of fans is likened to "worship." In the academic literature on celebrity culture, the argument that celebrity culture might have taken the place of religion, or indeed might actually be a kind of religion, is quite common. In his 1958 book *Christ and Celebrity Gods*,[2] Malcolm Boyd argues that through what he calls the "Age of Publicity" there is now a cult of the stars: "In the process of achieving pantheon status, we continually observe the mass media metamorphosis of the persons of these stars into legends." He then goes on to give examples from the pantheon, including Charles Lindbergh, J. P. Morgan, Babe Didrikson Zaharias, Ernest Hemingway, Billy Graham, Charles Chaplin, Greta Garbo, Mary Pickford, and Liberace.[3] Celebrities, Boyd observes, have become for us "symbols of various motifs of life." We have a kind of vicarious share in the lives of our idols. Even at times when the "idol" may attempt to take his or her own life, says Boyd, or indeed especially at such times, there may be forged "a strong, almost religious, tie between idol and idolater."[4]

The idea that a celebrity is some kind of near-god or idol has become a common theme. In popular culture, the use of the term "idol," such as in shows like *American Idol*, has become routine. The idea of celebrity as idol has also continued in academic literature. Gary Laderman of Emory University, for instance, writing more than fifty years after Boyd, sees celebrities as semireligious figures or false gods. "Celebrity icons," Laderman says, "arouse the religious passions of followers in modern society who find spiritual meaning, personal fulfilment, and awe-inspiring motivation in the presence of these idols." The first part of the twentieth century gave birth to what Laderman calls "new gods," who are worshipped on the "sacred altar" of celebrity culture. The religious practices associated with celebrity worship invest in "mythologies that promise immortality"; celebrity worship grants not only spiritual rewards but also the possibility of the "reformulation of personal moral values and ultimate concerns." All of this indicates that celebrities have "acquired a sacred standing in American religious life," and this has happened as what Laderman calls mainline Protestantism's "stranglehold" on public life has loosened. The decline in religious institutions has left a vacuum that is filled by contemporary media. This has not ushered in an expected secular age; "Instead, celebrities were deified by fans whose religious impulses and hungers remained active in that cultural field that could bring out the best, or the worst, in them."[5]

The idea that celebrity culture is in some way like religion, or like a false religion, is common. As Laderman says, "Celebrity culture, the cult of celebrity, celebrity worship—these and other phrases are regularly used to capture the elusive, irreducible power of celebrity in the present and recent past."[6] There are, however, significant problems with the idea that celebrity culture is a religion. Most definitions of religion rely on at least one of the following ideas: a belief in some kind of supernatural being, the power of religion to somehow shape and sustain a community or a church, or a religious object's meaningful purchase on people's lives. Celebrity culture in almost all of these respects falls significantly short of what most commentators seem to feel is required of a religion. There is no reference in celebrity culture to a transcendent other. There is no regular gathering or community of celebrity worshippers, and the extent to which celebrities may or may not be a resource for meaning making is less than clear. In fact, most people, even those who are closely involved in it, would not necessarily see celebrity worship as a religion. Celebrity culture is much too frivolous to be a religion. Of course, finding any kind of common definition for religion is problematic, but religions, if anything, seem to take themselves very seriously—and no one takes celebrity culture seriously.

THE PERSISTENCE OF RELIGIOUS METAPHOR

If celebrity culture is clearly not a religion, it still seems to be religious or have religious elements. One way of expressing this distinction is to talk about celebrity culture as a kind of religion or para-religion. The concept of para-religion seeks to draw a distinction between the persistence of the religious or the theological in the discourse of celebrity media and those ongoing characteristics and general "weight" and significance that traditional definitions would normally ascribe to religion. Religious imagery and metaphor appear with some regularity in the representation of celebrity. Celebrities seem to articulate or connect the possibilities of identity with echoes of the sacred. We speak of celebrities as screen goddesses or as legends or as icons because the religious analogy takes us into this sacred arena. The sacred here does not refer to any kind of transcendence. Instead, the sacred in celebrity culture refers to the self or rather the collective sum of the individual selves. This sacred self (or selves) is reflected back to the individual through the image of the celebrity. So celebrities are sacred figures that reflect versions of our own selves, painted as divine.

Ian Bradley of St. Andrews University makes a very similar observation about the prevalence of theological themes and spirituality in contemporary forms of musical theater: "As establishment religion and conventional church-going decline, perhaps it is not surprising that religious imagery and themes are surfacing more and more in the anti-establishment worlds of arts and entertainment. Musicals, with their cross-cultural appeal and strange mixture of commercial calculation and creative genius, are at the very heart of the new touchy-feely, up-front spirituality of post-modern society with its search for values, its quest for experience and sensation and its openness to a whole range of visual and aural stimuli."[7] It is in this context described by Bradley that the divinization of celebrity finds some purchase.

As divine and semidivine figures, celebrities might be compared to the gods, goddesses, mortals, and semidivine characters that are found in the myths of ancient Greece and Rome. Like the pantheon of ancient gods, our modern-day celebrities seem to represent the contradictions in what it means to be human. We are familiar with the concept that the ancient gods are both sublime and carnal. They are immortal, but they behave badly. Celebrities in similar ways combine the sacred and the profane (actually we could also add the inane). Celebrity culture therefore takes us into how popular culture negotiates the sacred to identify potentialities of the self. To speak of celebrity culture as a kind of theology therefore does not tell us anything about the Christian God, but it does reveal something of how we see ourselves.

THEMES IN A THEOLOGY OF THE SACRED SELF

As I have suggested, celebrity culture is not a "religion," but it does have religious elements. These "elements" operate primarily at the level of image and representation. They persist as an analogy that articulates theological themes or links up such themes to celebrity culture. Celebrity narratives make frequent use of theological terms and phrases, such as worship, icon, divinity, sin, fall, redemption, and salvation. These terms have been unhooked from their previous location in a largely Christian theological tradition and have been rearticulated with celebrities as symbols of the self. So theological themes are taken up and used to structure the way in which the media discuss celebrities' various cavortings, successes, and failures. The mix of the sacred and the profane then serves as a resource for the negotiation of identity in and through popular culture.

The theological metaphors and religious analogies in celebrity culture allow a glimpse into the processes of the sacralization of the self in popular culture. These metaphors and analogies are an aspect of what Paul Heelas and Linda Woodhead, both of Lancaster University, have called the "subjective turn in contemporary religion."[8] Religious metaphors as they appear in celebrity culture paint a picture of the possibilities of the sacred self. At the same time, as religious and theological metaphors are taken up and used in celebrity discourse, they undergo subtle but significant changes. So, for instance, the notion of "idol" carries with it a key theme in the theology of the sacred self: irony. To speak of idols is to invoke the inauthentic nature of celebrity worship. Celebrity culture invokes a knowing adoration of what are openly labeled as false gods. We are asked to worship versions of our sacred selves reflected through the lens of media-generated images, but we are always reminded that these are not really gods at all. What this reveals is the conflicted nature not only of our sense of self but also of our perception of the divine.

Confusion over the nature of the sacred is also seen in the variety of gods in the celebrity pantheon. Polytheism in celebrity worship signifies the extent to which we need a range of possibilities for the sacred self. Celebrity culture keeps the options open when it comes to gods. We are offered a choice of divinities and a menu for the sacred self. Our confusion over the choice of gods extends to what we expect of the sacred. Celebrity culture seems to revel not only in the celebration of the rise of mere mortals into celebrity gods but also in the seeming inevitability that these figures will fail. We find a particular pleasure in seeing our gods make mistakes. Paradoxically, it seems to confirm their "humanity." Nowhere is this more evident than in the way celebrity media seem to revel in the bad behavior of celebrities. Every day we are presented with an endless cavalcade of cheating sports personalities, unfaithful partners, and addicted stars and starlets. Yet this delight in gods who behave badly is writ through with a much deeper yearning for faithfulness, beautiful homes, and happy families. The "material" visions of the good life that celebrities seem to inhabit are predicated on the central importance of relationships and, above all, notions of fidelity. We may enjoy the prurient, but we are actually desperate for everyone to stick together. This is why we abhor the love rat and despise the person who has it all and seems to just throw it away.

The condemnation of celebrities who are tempted into "sin" takes us into the heart of the theology of the sacred self. We are the ones who judge. Magazines, newspapers, and Web sites are all vehicles for a popular inquisition. We have the all-seeing eye. We decide who goes and who stays. We sit in judgment on our own gods. And we judge our gods because they have so much and yet fail to "make the most of themselves"—a key value in celebrity worship. After all, if this is a religion of the sacred self, what greater apostasy could there be?

1

CELEBRITY WORSHIP

Michael Jackson was as contentious dead as he was in life. His death in Beverly Hills in 2009 was a news sensation. On the day he died, the search engine Google reacted to the sudden spike in activity as though to a virus attack as millions searched using the star's name. At the same time, the social networking and microblogging service Twitter was reported to have crashed due to a massive increase in Jackson-related posts.[1] Media organizations and newspapers around the world immediately switched to blanket coverage of the singer's life as they repeated the few facts that were then known about the circumstances surrounding his death. Yet despite evident interest in the story, after three days of Jackson headlines the head of the BBC Newsroom, Mary Hockaday, was forced to defend the corporation's coverage against widespread criticism. It wasn't simply that there were more important news stories: war in Afghanistan and conflict in Pakistan. It was the fact that Jackson was someone who divided opinion. As Hockaday said, "It is clear that Michael Jackson meant different things to different generations, both among our audiences and among our own staff. There are some who had followed him as a boy star, but there's also a large number of younger people who never saw him perform at his height but are only too aware of the controversy about his personal life and his increasingly eccentric appearance and behaviour."[2]

This wasn't the first time in the space of a year that the death of a celebrity caused problems for news organizations. A few weeks before, the BBC had once again been under fire in the British press for the headlines it had devoted to the death from cervical cancer of the *Big Brother* reality TV star Jade Goody. Jade, like Jackson, was also seen as a contentious figure. For many she represented the dumbing down of the mainstream media. Viewers wrote in to say that though it was obviously a very sad and untimely death, it was surely not worthy of being the main story on Britain's national broadcaster. The BBC defended the coverage, saying that there was huge public interest and that Jade had heightened awareness of the dangers of cervical cancer.[3] Jade, like Jackson, was a divisive figure. In death as in life, what they represented, and what they meant, was far from clear.

The obituary in the *Guardian* newspaper drew parallels between Jade Goody's funeral and that of Princess Diana. While it was admitted that thousands rather than millions lined the streets for Jade's funeral, the paper said that, "like a working-class Princess Diana, Jade became the object of strangers' intense feelings, and she became a sacrifice, a woman whose suffering and death made it possible for people to ritually cry for someone they scarcely knew."[4] As her cancer rapidly spread, each day the tabloid papers carried pictures of Jade, charting her approaching death. Writing in the *Independent*, Stephen Glover also drew the parallel with Princess Diana, the "people's princess." Diana may have been a member of the Royal Family, but she was seen as being "ordinary." Jade, Glover said, was the validation of the ordinary. Her story is proof that we do not need to be special to achieve what he calls the "secular state of grace which we know as celebrity."[5] Glover laments the way that the public, encouraged by the media, "worship the ordinary" through figures such as Princess Diana and Jade Goody. Words and phrases such as "ritual," "state of grace," "sacrifice," and indeed "worship" are an indication of the association that has been forged between celebrity culture and religious expression.

When Gods Die Young

In 2008 the actor Heath Ledger was found dead.[6] Within hours of his death, fans were creating a shrine to his memory outside the apartment in

Lower Manhattan where his body was discovered. The tributes included flowers, poems, pictures, and paintings.[7] Flowers and shrines have become a regular feature in the way that fans mark the death of a celebrity. Fifteen years after his death in April 1994, the rock singer Kurt Cobain was still mourned by people in his native Seattle, who continued to leave flowers at a park bench in Viretta Park.[8] Immediately following the announcement of Cobain's death, thousands of people gathered for a memorial to the singer. One fan, who was twenty-three when the singer died, remembered taking part in a service in Seattle Center. Cobain, she said, was valued in Seattle because "he was ours." "Nirvana," she explained, was "as important as Starbucks and Microsoft in making us count."[9]

The practices of laying flowers, lighting candles, and holding memorial services are a familiar reaction to the death of a celebrity. On one level they seem to form part of the usual rituals of death and grieving, but in celebrity worship these practices become articulated with inchoate expressions of the "sacred." An example of this is seen at the places of memorial linked to two previous rock stars, both of whom died before their time: Jim Morrison and Marc Bolan. Jim Morrison's grave in Père Lachaise Cemetery in Paris is one of the most visited tourist sites in the city. In her guide for students visiting the French capital, Kathleen Crisp speaks of "[f]ans and seekers still mak[ing] Paris Pilgrimages to the grave of Jim Morrison."[10] Here the rock fan is explicitly linked to the religious. Fans are tourists, but they may also be seekers who are on a kind of pilgrimage. A similar link between religious analogy and the practices of fans is evident in another "tourist guide," this time to obscure places in London. The Shady Old Lady's Guide to London tells us about a small side road in southwest London where the "faithful fans" still leave notes and flowers. This is the site where in 1977 the glam rock singer and guitarist Marc Bolan crashed his girlfriend's mini into a tree. Just as Crisp talks about pilgrimage, the London tourist guide calls the singer a "rock god" and the place of his fatal accident "Marc Bolan's Rock Shrine."[11]

When celebrities die young, religious imagery is often taken up and used to express the reactions of fans. In part this comes from the slight incongruity between the sense of loss that is being expressed and the fact that those grieving never knew the person who died. The grief is clearly real and in some cases enduring, but it also seems to be mysterious. When the rap artist Tupac Shakur was murdered in Las Vegas in 1996, writers from the Web site All Eyez on Me went onto the streets to gather reactions to his death. The fans expressed their feeling that Tupac was "one of them." He was important not simply because he was a rapper and famous but because of what he "meant." Fans mourned Tupac because of what he signified to them:

> DAPHNE, 36: We know what his music was about. Lot of people, some people don't. But we know his music was down for our people. We listen to it. We have it. We know the messages, y'know, the words that he's saying and everything. And, you know, we miss him. Its just like I'm losing a son.

> EMMITT, 22 (gesturing to a large tattoo on his stomach): That's for like, all the pain that we done went through. I suffered the same life he just suffered, living that street life, that thug life. All of it's real. Just 'cause you get famous don't mean nothing. Enemies still catch up with you.

> MAN 1: I looked up the night Tupac died, they pronounced him dead, and I seen one star in the sky and it was kind of hazy 'cause it was cloudy. but you know what I figured is that was Tupac . . . you know what I'm sayin'? That's how I looked at it.[12]

The reaction of the fans is more than shock at the violent death of a singer. The loss they feel seems to be very immediate. It comes out of a close identification with Tupac. Several years after Tupac's death, writing on the blog HELLOarticle.com, R. B. Riddle, the blogger, said that the rapper should be remembered because he was the spokesperson for a generation. Tupac could speak out because he had been exposed to many of the things that "we all experience." Tupac knew it because he had lived the life. We mourn Tupac because "Tupac was us. When he passed a part of us passed."[13]

The reaction of these rap fans is far from unusual. In 1980 Tom Brook was the first British reporter to arrive outside the Dakota Building in New York on the evening singer and former Beatles member John Lennon was murdered. Twenty years later, writing for BBC

News Online, the entertainment correspondent described a scene where bewildered and grief-struck people slowly gathered together. Some held candles. A woman sang the Lennon song "Give Peace a Chance." Lennon fan Mitch Weiss remembered the night as one where so many were grieving, "The whole street was filled with people, all ages, all descriptions, in groups, individually, many of them sobbing, curious onlookers, reporters, and just a lot of people in a state of shock."[14] Brook recalls that his reports had to be recorded and sent back to London in a kind of mechanical way because he felt it difficult to keep his own emotions under check. For the previous generation, he recalls, the death of President Kennedy was the "truly seismic event." For the baby boomers it was the death of John Lennon.[15] The mourning of Lennon continues into the present with the establishment of the Strawberry Fields memorial in Central Park, New York, close to the site where he was shot. Fans still visit the site, leaving poems, flowers, and candles.

The sense of loss and public grief that is seen in the mourning for John Lennon and pop stars such as Michael Jackson and Tupac Shakur is not at all unique. In 1926 the film star Rudolph Valentino died at the age of thirty-one while undergoing surgery. When it became known that his body would be embalmed and people could come to his New York funeral and pay their respects, thousands began to gather. It was reported that seventy-five people an hour processed by the coffin. By the end of the first day, fifty thousand people had passed through the funeral home. The fans who came to view the body were said to have been in many cases "frenzied." People fainted and sobbed openly, while many others touched or even kissed the casket.[16] For Gary Laderman, these displays of devotion seem to show an attachment to Valentino that went beyond expectations. The behavior of these "stunned followers" is either some new form of religion or it is a kind of pathology.[17] The celebrity represents a value or a collective memory that could be seen as being in some way "sacred." Here again, this is not necessarily a religion as such, but it is an indication that some kind of convergence is taking place between religious sensibilities and practices and popular culture.

Sudden death lays bare the depth of feeling that people have for celebrities. When gods die young, celebrity worship becomes explicit and takes to the streets. The adoration of fans is mixed with practices that are akin to religion. The adoption of religious imagery and metaphors for celebrity worship, however, does not necessarily point to a "beyond" or a transcendent other. Even more surprising is that what is being mourned is not simply a great artist or an amazing pop singer. Who the person was and what that person did does not quite explain the reaction that people have when a celebrity dies. After all, film stars, rappers, and rock singers are basically entertainers, but what grieving seems to indicate is that celebrities carry a significance that is beyond their profession or indeed their individuality. Public grief reveals the "meaningfulness" or the collective significance of a celebrity. This significance has its origins not so much in who the celebrity is or even what he or she has done but in what the celebrity represents to fans. It is the collective "us" in the celebrity that is being worshipped. So celebrities are "deities" only to the extent that they are carrying the projected identifications of fans.

Worshipping Diana

The public reaction to the 1997 death of Princess Diana took everyone by surprise. The 2006 movie *The Queen*, starring Helen Mirren, beautifully captures the extent to which the British establishment and especially the Royal Family were wrong-footed by a rather "un-British" expression of public grief. After the event, academics were still scratching their heads trying to make sense of what had happened on the streets of London. In the book *Diana: The Making of a Media Saint*, scholars try to understand the outpouring of grief that they had not only witnessed but actually been a part of, either through the media or by visiting Kensington Palace themselves. Jack O'Sullivan argues that the funeral of Diana showed what he calls "post-Christian Britain out in force."[18] He suggests that, just as there was a marked distinction between the British people and those in Buckingham Palace, there was also a difference between the people on the street and those inside the walls of Westminster Abbey. "People have a new religion," says O'Sullivan. "Most did not gather outside the Abbey and Kensington Palace to find God. They came together for a more internal exercise, to explore their all important inner selves and feelings, an event prompted by the death of a woman who excelled in expressing her own emotions."[19] Ian Jack is less convinced. The mourning of Diana, he says, is "recreational grieving." The crowd is enjoying being together; this is "grief-lite," according to Jack.[20] Others argues that the public grieving at Diana's funeral revealed a certain English reserve. They point out that there were really very few people breaking down during the funeral; rather, there was an uncanny silence. So they suggest that the flowers and the teddy bears were a symbol of grief rather than emotionality itself.[21] Even the Church of England was divided over the significance of Diana's death. Then-Archbishop George Carey rather optimistically asserted that the "humbling and astonishing reaction" to the death of the princess revealed a "continuing and deep respect for the Churches,"[22] while the bishop of Rochester, Michael Nazir-Ali, was uncharacteristically more measured, suggesting that the public displays of grief revealed a spiritual feeling or an implicit Christianity that was the churches' task to make explicit.[23]

Like many others, the cultural critic Judith Williamson cried when she heard the news of Diana's death that Sunday morning. This, she felt, was a senseless accident that took the life of an already vulnerable woman and left two young sons to face a life of public duty on their own. Walking around the mountains of flowers that were left outside Kensington Palace and reading the notes and poems that were left with them, she was again moved to tears. Williamson did not doubt the feelings expressed, yet she observed how these messages were written to someone who, though absent through her death, was also in a sense never present, or at least never present to those who were grieving.[24] She suggests that people live their emotional lives through celebrities like Diana "by proxy."[25] Diana's death, Williamson says, "destabilised familiar meanings, both because of its unpredictability (it was not a plot move we saw coming) and because it removed the real person behind the images, so that they were suddenly simply images—as if paper money was suddenly revealed as just paper."[26] Diana had been so omnipresent in our culture. Her image was always with us in such a way that the absence of Diana was hard to grasp, almost unthinkable. Thus, says Williamson, the public mourning at places like Kensington Palace represented an attempt to grab hold of the concrete in the midst of uncertainty.

Writing before Diana's death, the American cultural critic and academic Camille Paglia argued that the iconography of Princess Diana situated her as a divine archetype. Diana, Paglia suggested, was one of the most powerful images in popular culture, a case study of "the modern cult of celebrity." Diana, Paglia said, demonstrates the way that celebrity worship stimulates "atavistic religious emotions."[27] Diana's story taps into deep archetypes in our culture that demonstrate that the power of the woman has not disappeared. According to Paglia, Diana's husband Charles had sought a Protestant virgin to be his bride, only to find that "his philandering attempts to remain himself produced a new Catholic Madonna, a modern Mary with a taste for rock and roll."[28] Diana, she says, radiates a magnetic power. Her extraordinary worldwide popularity shows the endurance of "hierarchy." This is a power, says Paglia, that "fashionable academic paradigms—influenced by feminism, Marxism, Foucault and the Frankfurt School—cannot understand and whose enduring mystique can only be explained by Roman Catholicism and Hollywood history."[29] Paglia's point is very suggestive. It indicates how the metaphor of religion and the idea of worship describe how celebrity culture, while it may not strictly be religion, appears to carry within it some connection to the sacred. So the metaphor of worship allows the commentator to explore this specifically "religious" terrain. In the events in London at the time of Diana's death, we are given a glimpse of the extent to which the observations of Paglia and others seem to be more substantial than mere journalistic rhetoric.

When those working in the media reach for a metaphor for the celebrity phenomenon, some kind of religious analogy is never far away. Faced with the massive media event that surrounded the death of Michael Jackson or the unprecedented outpouring of grief that was seen on the streets of London when Princess Diana was killed, the idea of celebrity "worship" seems to be a plausible and rather compelling explanation. Searching for a reason why figures such as Jade Goody and the pantheon of mortals, gods, and demigods whose omnipresence has spread from publications such as *Hello!*, the *National Enquirer*, and *People* magazine to our national TV news, commentators often resort to "religion" as a loose analytical category. As Cooper Lawrence, the author of *The Cult of Celebrity*, says, "Few can resist the attraction of our glamorous twenty-first-century gods and goddesses."[30] The cumulative effect of the coverage of celebrity culture might leave the impression that we are all to some extent in thrall to this "cult." But this is far from the case, for while there may be many believers, there are also a great many who refuse to bow the knee.

Celebrity worship is a conflicted and contested religion (if indeed it is a religion at all). Among the news media there are those who feel they must apologize for the attention they are giving to celebrities. It appears that those at the heart of the "cult" are often in two minds as to the real significance of celebrity figures such as Michael Jackson, Jade Goody, or Princess Diana. This ambivalence actually replicates the way that many of us are divided over our interest in celebrities. We seem to have "half an eye" on their antics. We are worshippers with short attention spans and a tendency toward a slightly cynical take on the characters that fill our news media. We disagree with enthusiasts such as Lawrence; we can take or leave, and in most cases leave, celebrity culture. We don't see ourselves as part of any "cult." Yet we know that this "worship" is out there. We seem to know about these "celebs." We may not choose to worship, but somehow we are aware that the "images" of the gods and goddesses of the celebrity cult have imprinted themselves on our consciousness. We feel that we know these people. Occasionally we take notice when they cheat on their partner, have a car crash, adopt a baby, or tell us we should be saving the rain forest. We pretend that we have no interest in where they eat out, if they get drunk, or if they change their hairstyle or their religion, but somehow we know when these things take place. So many of us are like nonbelievers living in a devotedly Catholic country. We know that every now and then the streets will be filled with worshippers. We see the statues and the images paraded at major festivals. This is not our own form of worship, but we may well accept that this religious environment has an effect upon us, even if that effect is negative. Celebrity worship in much the same way forms part of the world that we inhabit. Celebrity worship appears to be a kind of religion that is "in the air," but if it is religion, it is a religion that has its dissenters and Dawkins-esque critics. Perhaps this is simply a confirmation that the cult of celebrity is indeed religion!

A "Kind of" Worship

Michael Jackson's death sparked a renewed discussion concerning "celebrity worship." Jackson was widely seen as a modern-day icon. This view of the singer persisted even during his trial for child abuse, during which some expected his "iconic status" might be questioned or at least tempered a little. ABC News was not alone in marveling at the continuing devotion of Jackson's fans, who appeared to demonstrate a kind of religious belief. The persistence of their faith in Michael Jackson, said the news organization, was a kind of "fan worship."[31] For some religious commentators, the iconic status of Michael Jackson and the devotion of his fans became a target for attack. Quoting the Qur'an, blogger Ibrahim Ramey compared the fans' devotion to Jackson to the worship of the one true God. Ramey acknowledged the importance of Michael Jackson, especially for African Americans, and he recognized the significance of Jackson's musical achievement, yet he argued that it is wrong to treat a human being as being worthy of worship. With what might be seen as a grim theological observation, Ramey said that Jackson was now facing his maker. In time, Ramey said, each one of us will be called to judgment, and then we will all have to account for our participation in celebrity worship.[32] The comments by Ramey and others in the media did not go unnoticed by Jackson fans.

The idea of worship and "devotion" to Michael was discussed on the Michael Jackson Fan Club Web site. "You know what's strange about this?" said one of the fans posting on the site, "For me anyways? Michael was the biggest star in the world . . . but I never looked at him as 'Michael Jackson—a celebrity. He's Mike, it's been like a kinship. I'm sure someone has to know what I mean. p.s. I think he'd be horrified at being 'idolized' or worshiped."[33] So for some fans at least, the notion of "worship" was disputed. They might self-identify as fans and even regard Jackson as a kind of "relative," but they could shy away from a specifically religious understanding of their devotion.

A certain ambivalence or ambiguity is a characteristic of the cult of celebrity. Elements of celebrity worship appear to be "like religion," while at the same time those most closely involved may well deny that their interest in a celebrity is in any way religious. Chris Rojek sees this kind of ambiguity as part of a much larger process of secularization. Celebrity worship, he argues, is a symptom of the changing nature of religion. In secularized societies the sacred becomes disconnected from religious traditions and is relocated in what Rojek calls "mass media celebrities." So he suggests that in secularization, worship and the religiously meaningful are reconnected with these media-generated figures. The new religious environment finds celebrities becoming objects of "cult worship."[34] Classically, secularization describes the way that religion is subject to processes of institutional decline and deregulation, but these forces have not led to the replacement of religion by scientific or rationalizing systems, as had been expected. Instead of being replaced entirely, the religious has actually been relocated. The disconnection of the sacred from specifically religious traditions means that religion is now found in association with nature and with culture, and in particular popular culture. Thus it is possible to detect what Rojek calls "an intense collective effervescence" in ecological movements and among animal rights activists, as well as in spectator sports. All of this suggests that there is now a "substantial convergence" between religion and popular culture.[35]

Celebrity culture is one of the places where this convergence between religion and popular culture is evident. It is not so much that celebrity culture is actually religion; neither is it a substitute for religion. Instead, according to Rojek, "it is the milieu in which religious recognition and belonging are now enacted."[36] Celebrity culture might operate as a "moral equivalence" to the worship of God. Such equivalence means that "celebrity culture is now ubiquitous, and establishes the main scripts, presentational props, conversational codes and other source materials through which cultural relations are constructed."[37] Thus there are some parallels between the ways that religion and celebrity culture operate as structuring mechanisms in society. Yet, says Rojek, organized religion presents an ordered view of the social and the spiritual, while celebrity culture is incapable of such a project. If celebrity worship is in some way religious, then it is a religion that, while it may inspire intense devotion and compelling feelings of identification, is "basically a fragmented, unstable culture that is unable to sustain an encompassing, grounded view of social and spiritual order."[38] At the same time, with the decline of traditional religious institutions, Rojek concludes, celebrity worship is one of the ways that the religious persists. It is what he calls a "replacement strategy."[39] So celebrity worship is a kind of religion or it is related in some ways to religion. It is a displaced or a replaced form of the religious in secularization, but it is also dissimilar to religion because it is not a formal system that can order society and structure institutions.

Types of Worship

The sudden death of a celebrity seems to bring religious elements of celebrity culture to the forefront. These elements do not comprise an actual religion, but religious analogies are often used to explain the various ways that people respond to celebrities, and "celebrity worship" has become a popular shorthand for these kinds of behaviors. But celebrity worship is not just a way for the popular press to talk about fans. A number of academic studies by psychologists examine the phenomenon of celebrity worship. To describe a cluster of behaviors, these research projects use the specific idea that fans "worship" celebrities. From these observations, researchers have devised a scale to measure the intensity and extent to which fans engage in worship. They call this the "celebrity worship scale."

The celebrity worship scale is used to measure the psychological implications of celebrity worship. The scale is based on previous research that indicated that celebrity worship or "appreciation" can be divided into two broad categories with associated "personality differences." The first category represents mild or nonpathological forms of celebrity worship. This category includes those who belong to fan clubs. These clubs appear to cater to fans who are more introverted, and researchers observe that individuals in these groups tend to "report fewer and less intimate relationships" than they did before becoming a fan.[40] The second group consists of individuals who are engaged in more extreme or pathological forms of celebrity worship, including stalking, erotomania, and inappropriate correspondence with celebrities. Here psychological disorders may include "issues of trust and a faulty capacity to maintain relationships."[41] The researchers found through the use of the scale that celebrity worship fit into three, rather than two, broad categories. In the first category, low-level worship, they noted individualistic behaviors such as watching, reading, and keeping up with celebrity narratives. The second category includes more social activities, such as watching and talking about celebrities with other fans, and the third category involves a heightened empathy as fans tend to overidentify with celebrities.[42] So while at the lowest levels of celebrity worship the activities are rather solitary, toward the higher levels there appears to be an increased sociality; then at the very highest level there is a return to the private sphere.[43] These findings on celebrity worship are developed in two further psychological studies. The first found that celebrity worship that was engaged in for intense personal reasons was associated with poor mental health, including neuroticism, worry, anxiety, and depression.[44] The second study, which made use of a further-revised form of the celebrity worship scale, discovered body image–related mental health issues, but only among women.[45]

In the present context, the exact findings are less significant, perhaps, than the more obvious point that psychologists are able to identify something that they call celebrity worship. This means that in a scientific context researchers have not only shown that particular practices and behaviors make up the worship of celebrities but that these behaviors have measurable effects on the lives of individuals. These findings in themselves do not necessarily show that there is anything specifically religious taking place in these behaviors. The researchers appear to have adopted the term "worship" because it suggests a kind of attachment or affiliation that is "like religion." Nevertheless, these findings are suggestive of the presence in these behaviors of something that is akin to religion.

Just as psychological academic research has identified the existence of celebrity worship, the adoration of the fan has a long history as a significant phenomenon in the quite different field of film studies. Film critics and popular media have quite commonly used the analogy of worship to describe the "religious" hold that stars have over their audiences. The French film critic Edgar Morin, writing in the 1970s, described the worship of the star as a kind of cult:

> Worshipped as heroes, divinized, the stars are more than objects of admiration. They are also subjects of a cult. A religion in embryo has formed around them. This religion diffuses its frenzies over most of the globe. No one who frequents the dark auditoriums is really an atheist. But among the movie going masses can be distinguished the sect of the faithful who wear relics and otherwise consecrate themselves to worship, the fanatics, the fans.[46]

In his book *Mythologies*, Roland Barthes connects fan worship to the symbolic significance of Greta Garbo's face in the film *Queen Christina*.

Garbo, he says, offers to the gaze a kind of platonic idea of the human face. Her name, "the divine," does not convey a superior state of beauty; rather, what is seen is "her corporeal person, descended from a heaven where all things are formed and perfected in the clearest light."[47] The cult of the fan, says Morin, consists of specialist magazines which produce what he calls the "vivifying elements of their faith."[48] Photographs, pilgrimages, ceremonies, festivals, and correspondence clubs facilitate the adoration of the fan worshipper.[49] For Morin the "star" is like the patron saint to which the fan must dedicate himself or herself. To be faithful, he says, is to "consume" and thus "assimilate" the saint/star. Assimilation is effected through information. This is not an ordered or analytic knowledge of the star; rather, it is comprised of snapshots, gossip, rumors, and "indiscretions in a delectable engluttening."[50] Here in film studies the idea of religion is used a metaphor to describe in a vivid way the relationship between film audiences and the stars to whom they are devoted. The metaphor is pursued with some vigor, and yet even here the idea that what is being described is a "religion" in a formal sense is open to question.

FANS WHO WORSHIP

The analogous use of the word "worship" suggests that, while we may not be dealing with a religion in a traditional sense, celebrity culture does appear to be "religious." From psychology it is evident that the idea of worship indicates a level of identification that might in some cases be pathological. The semiotic discussion of the significance of the film star or a figure such as Princess Diana indicates that a religious metaphor allows the appreciation of some kind of "sacred" in popular culture. The idea of worship or religious regard is part of the etymology of the word "fan." Ellis Cashmore, in his book *Celebrity/Culture* suggests that the notion of the "fan" has two main roots. The first traces the word "fan" to the latin *fanaticus,* meaning "of the temple": so the fan is one who is "excessively enthusiastic" or taken up with a zeal that is most usually seen in "religious fervour."[51] The second root is linked to the world of prizefighting in the nineteenth century, in which one who supported a particular fighter was referred to as a "fancy."[52] The links to popular culture and boxing are a significant reminder that while celebrity worship may hint at the sacred, it is always to some extent tinged with the profane. At the same time, while for most fans celebrity worship may be rather distant from their idea of the religion, there are fan groups whose practices and behaviors appear to blur the distinction between popular culture and religion, making the convergence between the religious and media-generated popular culture much more evident.

The International Group of the Anointed Michael Followers announced itself via the online social network Facebook as the new religion of the "trilenium."[53] The followers claimed to worship Michael Jackson not because he was ordinary but because he was extraordinary. In fact, they believed that he was an angel trapped inside human flesh. The followers reportly believe that Michael Jackson is also a unique being: "Michael represents the hopes and dreams that live in each and every one of us, and [his] exceptional personality is the source to his constant media bashing and character assassination. Even though we're aware that he's physically human, the wholesome of his existence drives us to believe that he's spiritually divine."[54] The Web site CelebrityFIX.com refers to these Michael Jackson fans as nutcases but quips that if they ever manage to start a church the music will be great.[55]

Elvis fans may not have exactly started a church, but in her research on Elvis Erica Doss has charted the various ways "religion-like" activities have become associated with the star. These include practices of collecting, arranging, and displaying pictures and images of Elvis and other Elvis-related memorabilia. Often these objects are arranged in a special Elvis room or an Elvis shrine.[56] Fans describe these rooms as places where they can be really close to Elvis or spend time alone with him. Fan Kim Epperley of Roanoke, Virginia, is quoted by Doss as saying that she likes to "go to her Elvis room down in the basement after supper. It's a quiet space and time for me."[57] The members of the MacLeod family call themselves "The Worlds Number 1 Elvis fans." They have transformed their entire home into a memorial to Elvis, crammed with Elvis images and related objects. They call this shrine Graceland Too, and they have opened it to the public. The MacLeods' introduction to those who visit their home explains their motivation: "While you are taking a tour of 'Graceland Too,' you are reliving his (Elvis') life, you also see what has made our lives complete, in doing what we love to do. Paul and Elvis Aaron Presley MacLeod have given up all they had in life to find their passion and live out their dreams daily by being surrounded by the image, voice and eternal flame of Elvis Aaron Presley. ELVIS WILL NEVER LEAVE THIS BUILDING AS HE WILL NEVER LEAVE OUR HEARTS!!!"[58] Building a shrine to Elvis Presley clearly has religious parallels. This impression is reinforced by the practices and beliefs associated with these spaces. These practices are suggested in language expressing closeness to Elvis or the idea that he will always be in the fans' hearts and never leave them.

In Australia, researchers found that members of the fan club for the British pop singer Cliff Richard reported intense relationships to their favorite star. Like Elvis fans, Cliff fans also seem to have a sense that the singer is always with them in every aspect of their lives. As one fan said, "You feel you know him. He's a bit like an extension of your family. When we went to the airport to see Cliff arrive I took my young son. He ran up under everyone's legs right up to Cliff and asked him for a kiss and a cuddle. He just sees him as an extension of the family, because Cliff is always present in our home."[59] When researchers asked how fans would respond if they did not have Cliff in their lives, the response was one of deep shock. One fan is reported to have responded by saying, "I'd be devastated. Our lives would be poorer. We have so many memories. He's part of our lives and part of us."[60] Just as in Doss' work on Elvis fans, the researchers in Australia found that many of the female fans had rooms in their homes that were devoted to Cliff. These rooms were filled with memorabilia and pictures of their favorite star. The Cliff Richard Fan Club appeared to offer a means for affiliation and sharing. As one respondent explained, "Knowing that you were able to share with like minds it was great to have someone to talk to about Cliff."[61]

Fan clubs are not only places of identity and belonging—they may also become a focus for practices that have other religious similarities. A good example of this is Elvis Week, which is held every August in Memphis. Elvis Week reaches its culmination in an all-night candle-light vigil on the anniversary of Elvis' death at Graceland. The vigil was started a year after Elvis' death by the Elvis Country Fan Club of Dallas, and it has continued ever since. The ritual starts with members of the Country Fan Club reading poems and singing songs. Then a procession passes between rows of fan club members who stand with their heads bowed, lining the driveway into Graceland. The visitors slowly make their way to the Meditation Garden. Each visitor carries a candle lit from a single torch at the start of the procession. The ritual comes to a close only when every visitor has had a chance to pause briefly at the resting place of the star in the Meditation Garden.[62] The practices and rituals associated with Elvis Week are clearly very reminiscent of religion. Fan groups do not only replicate the kind of affiliation characteristic of many religions, they also appear to appropriate rituals such as processions and the construction of sacred spaces. This kind of displaced religion that merges with popular culture might be seen as the more extreme end of celebrity worship, but as psychological research has shown, the various practices that are seen as forms of celebrity worship create a kind of continuum. Yet even at this very extreme end of celebrity culture it is hard to identify a formal or traditional kind of "religion." Instead, it seems that "religion-like" activities are being appropriated in much the same way that religious and theological metaphors such as "icon" and "idol" are used in celebrity discourse.

PARA-SOCIAL INTERACTIONS

In the practice of fans we see a "kind of" religious behavior, a religion that isn't a religion and a religious gathering that isn't quite a church. This "kind of" religion or para-religion has a number of similarities with the way that fans form social relationships with celebrities. Such a relationship is intense, but of course it is a relationship with someone whmo most fans have never met. These are relationships that are not really relationships; they are "para-social." The concept of the para-social was developed in the 1950s when the researchers Donald Horton and R. Richard Wohl identified a kind of "para-social interaction" taking place between television viewers and TV personalities.[63] They observed the way that audiences appeared to form "friendships" with the characters they were watching on their televisions. These unusual attachments were focused on both fictional (e.g., a character in drama series) and nonfictional figures (e.g., newsreaders or weather presenters). In interviews, some viewers expressed not only positive but also negative feelings about these characters. The negative feelings were often so strong that viewers would say that they "hated" a particular TV character. The research uncovered how TV viewing led to a sense of familiarity and to feelings of intimacy with the characters that filled the screen, but these relationships were one way. Viewers "knew" the characters on TV, but these were people they had never met. So there were identifiable social elements to the relationship between viewers and TV personalities, but this sociality was limited. These limited social elements were labeled by the researchers as "para-social interactions."[64]

Versions of the para-social thesis have been variously used in understanding celebrity culture. The original thesis has been criticized because of a tendency to overpathologize the relationship between the fan and the celebrity to the extent that the relationship between fans and TV personalities is seen as being potentially abnormal. The research was apparently overconcerned with the possibility that para-social connections will generate an obsessive pursuit of direct relationship.[65] For later cultural commentators the relationship between fans and celebrities is seen in more positive ways. For Chris Rojek, the idea of para-social interaction describes "relations of intimacy constructed through the mass-media rather than direct experience and face to face meetings."[66] He accepts that this is a kind of second-order relationship, but he also argues that for many isolated people a sense of intimacy with media figures is a vital support. There is an important difference, he argues, between the media coverage of celebrity in the present and in the 1950s, when the idea of para-social interaction was first developed. This difference relates to the range, the amount, and the overwhelmingly personal nature of the stories, pictures, and other media content. Specifically, Rojek says, "A peculiar tension in celebrity culture is that the physical and social remoteness of the celebrity is compensated for by the glut of mass-media information, including fanzines, press-stories, TV documentaries, interviews, newsletters and biographies, which personalize the celebrity, turning a distant figure from a stranger into a significant other."[67]

The significance of a distant "significant other" may go some way to explain the public mourning and rituals of grief that took place in London and elsewhere when Princess Diana died. These events, says Graeme Turner, are a prime example of the way that we form para-social interactions with celebrities. Turner rejects the idea that para-social interactions are some form of compensation for changes in communities' social organizations or that they are "impoverished substitutes" for "real" social relationships. The widespread reactions to the deaths of figures such as Elvis Presley, John Lennon, and Princess Diana demonstrate that there may be more meaningful patterns of significance at play in the para-social.[68] These were occasions, says Turner, when thousands of people all over the world appeared to respond with "real" emotion to the death of a person whom they knew only through the media. He accepts that the meaning of these mass expressions of grief is far from clear, but if we are to understand them, he argues, we must first accept at "face value" the testimony of those involved.[69] Similarly, for Cashmore, the idea of the para-social relationship "captures the way we think and feel about people we don't know and who don't know us but sometimes and unwittingly and unknowingly move us to act, occasionally in erratic and irrational ways."[70] Turner and Cashmore agree that these kinds of one-way relationships are nevertheless significant. For the fan, one-way para-social interactions are still felt as genuine; in fact, such interactions are so common they are hard to avoid. "Even if we wanted to insulate ourselves for a while," says Cashmore, "we couldn't escape over-hearing chats, glancing at newspaper or magazine covers, or resisting switching on the TV, even if only for the news."[71] Para-social interactions are an intimacy that is "at a distance."[72]

WORSHIP AND IDENTIFICATION

Despite the apparent significance of the celebrity-fan relationship, celebrity worship is adoration that is conducted at a distance; it is para-social in nature. Yet events such as the death of Diana demonstrate the extent to which certain celebrity figures carry an enduring symbolic significance. This significance is an indication that the relationship that people have with celebrities may operate as a source of identification and indeed identity. Turner supports this view, arguing that celebrity culture is now one of the main resources for the construction of the self: "As the media plays an ever more active role in the production of identity; as our consumption practices increasingly reflect choices that privilege the performance of identity; and as celebrity becomes an increasingly common component of media content; it is not surprising that celebrity

should become one of the primary locations where the news and entertainment media participate in the construction of cultural identity."[73]
The relationship between cultural identity and the celebrity, however,
is not always straightforward. As we have noted, the deaths of Michael
Jackson and Jade Goody revealed something of this complexity. The
division over the media coverage of the deaths of these two celebrities
demonstrates how celebrities mean different things to different people.
In fact, individuals may even feel conflicted in their own views of a
particular celebrity. This kind of ambivalent or conflicted relationship
between the fan and the celebrity can be described as a tension between
"identification" and "disidentification."[74]

Celebrity worship seems to operate in a complex field where individuals may in turns identify or disidentify with celebrities. Turner emphasizes
the "playfulness" in the cultural consumption of celebrities. He argues that
the construction of identity is as much play as it is work. As he puts it,
"When a women's magazine offers its readers advice on how to 'celebritize'
their wardrobe, then it is important to recognise that this offer is likely to
produce a playful and imaginative form of cultural consumption."[75] Fans
have a "give and take" with a range of media figures. Fans relate to celebrities by including them in the construction of "imaginary worlds." These
behaviors are not obsessive or pathological; rather, they show how individual celebrity worshippers may be acting with intelligence, wit, and a
measure of skepticism. Fans enjoy the connections that exist between gossip, information, and experiences. These together form a kind of web that
they are able to weave from entertainment programming, sports shows,
news, and advertising.[76] In these ways, individuals develop with celebrities relationships that form a part of their daily lives. This kind of intimacy
can be seen as both enriching and rewarding.

Identification does not necessarily imply a kind of power imbalance
where fans are "influenced" by media-generated celebrities. Fraser and
Brown, for instance, suggest that the relationships between fans and
celebrities are in fact defined by fans themselves: "Fans develop self-
defining relationships with celebrities and seek to adopt their perceived
attributes, resulting in powerful forms of personal and social transformation."[77] So the adoration of the fan in celebrity worship involves a
para-social relationship that is potentially transformative for the indi-

vidual. The connection between the fan and the celebrity goes a long way beyond identification. Celebrity worship, the act of being a fan, involves the appropriation of the celebrity as "part of the publicly performed self." So in adoration and worship, fans are seen to be shaping their sense of themselves through the "object of their fandom." The object of adoration, be it an individual celebrity, a TV show, a CD, or a sports team, is more than simply a possession: it becomes part of the fan's sense of himself or herself and also how he or she is viewed by others.[78]

Yet the notion of identification can be exaggerated. In his research into how the fame industry operates in Hollywood, Joshua Gamson divides fans into three groups based on their response to celebrity culture: believers, hipsters, and game players. The believers, he says, read celebrity narratives as if they portray some kind of reality concerning the star. Hipsters, meanwhile, are antibelievers who treat all media output as a kind of fiction. The majority of the audience, however, are what Gamson calls "game players."[79] This group reads celebrity culture on their own terms. They acknowledge and enjoy playing with the blurred language. For this group celebrity is not seen as a way to order values or find a sense of how to rank lifestyle and taste. Neither is it an ever-changing resource for identity choices; instead, they see celebrity-watching as a kind of tourist circuit or a game.[80] This idea of game playing tempers claims about the significance of celebrity to identity formation. At the same time, the critics of celebrity culture appear to miss the mark when they focus on the compensatory nature of celebrity worship. To suggest that celebrity watchers are embracing the superficial and therefore the socially ephemeral and insignificant is to fail to understand how this culture operates. Fans are meeting their social "needs" not so much through imaginary relationships to celebrities as through their relationships with other fans. It is the social relationships between fans as they interact, whether online or face to face, that are of primary significance.[81]

Gamson's work is an important corrective to claims concerning the importance of celebrities for the construction of the self. He shows how the symbolic significance of celebrities is mediated in and through the social relationships that fans themselves generate. This means that the relations that grow out of an event such as Elvis Week may be of more significance socially than the actual celebrity. At the same time, the notion of game playing and indeed the antibelief of the hispster serve to further temper ideas of identification. The para-social nature of celebrity worship therefore shows the complexity of the relationships that form a celebrity culture. This complexity has some parallels with religion. Through identification, celebrities, just like religious figures, may serve as a focus for identity construction and transformation. At the same time, disidentification points to the way that many of us are conflicted in our consumption of celebrity; yet for all those who reject celebrity there are those who seem to knowingly embrace its superficiality as a form of a game. This has implications for any attempt to read celebrity worship as a formal religion, since it would seem that the mixture of the sacred and the profane in celebrity culture extends to the reactions of the worshippers themselves.

Is Elvis a God?

The cult of the celebrity is religiously ambiguous. For some, the use of the terms "celebrity worship" or "adoration" moves beyond a simple analogy into more specifically religious claims. Rojek argues that the tension between the distance of the celebrity and the way the presence and influence of that figure is mediated through popular culture suggests a similarity with religion: "The tension has inescapable parallels with religious worship and these are reinforced by the attribution by fans of magical or extraordinary powers to the celebrity. Celebrities are thought to possess God-like qualities by some fans, while others— experiencing the power of celebrity to arouse deep emotions—recognise the spirit of the shaman." Rojek's thesis, that there are significant shamanic elements in celebrity culture, may well be overplayed, but another of his arguments—that celebrity worship is a form of displaced religion that carries some but not all of the characteristics of religion—is very helpful.

John Frow's article "Is Elvis a God?" deals directly with the religious significance of celebrity worship. Frow discusses the extent to which the practices and para-social interactions between fans and Elvis might or might not be considered a kind of religion. According to his own criteria, Frow comes to the conclusion that in many respects Elvis fans do indeed appear to behave as if they are engaged in some kind of religious practice. So to the extent that Elvis seems to have attracted a cult, Elvis should indeed be considered a god.[82] Frow's purpose is not so much to examine the relations between mass representation and religious experience as to explore what this kind of study might entail. He suggests that cultural studies have tended to ignore, or to have problems in theorizing, religion. "Religion is an embarrassment to us," says Frow, "it is an embarrassment to me, above all because we Western intellectuals are so deeply committed to the secularization thesis which makes religion an archaic remnant which ought to have withered away."[83] He makes a link between an appreciation of the religious in popular culture and the growing acceptance in his native Australia that it was a deep mistake for intellectuals and Western society to ignore the power and value of Aboriginal spirituality.[84]

However respectful such an approach might be, the mere idea that Elvis is God may not be received very kindly by Elvis fans. Doss found that when his fans were asked directly about the religious dimensions of Elvis they were very likely to be dismissive and indeed quite indignant. As one fan wrote, "Elvis did not die for our sins, nor is he Jesus Christ and it is very wrong to even try and draw comparisons."[85] Those interviewed by Doss argued that it was simply the media that were exaggerating the interest in Elvis as a religious figure. Doss' interview subjects were clear that most "normal fans" had no interest in the subject. Very similar objections were found in the research into the Sydney-based Cliff Richard Fan Club. Here many of the respondents were identified as "devout Christians," a trait they share with their chosen celebrity. The researcher observed that "[m]ost view Cliff as human rather than god-like."[86] The "most" in this sentence is highly suggestive. It indicates how celebrity worship is a fluid and ambiguous construct. Doss observes similar ambiguity among U.S.-based Elvis fans, many of whom would identify themselves as evangelical Christians or Roman Catholics. Doss argues that Elvis rooms and the shrines and rituals she observed during Elvis Week seem to indicate that for many fans Elvis is a powerful figure but that his influence is "mediated" by their particular theological commitments. This works, says Doss, because "images of Elvis are multifaceted, mercurial, and mysterious, and because American religiosity is essentially flexible and democratic. On the one level then, fans place their faith in images of Elvis because they correspond to the personal mores and ecclesiastical self-image they desire. On another level, fans place their faith in images of Elvis because he pro- vides a kind of 'secular spiritual succour,' because he can minister to their pleasure and their pain."[87]

CELEBRITY WORSHIP AS A "KIND OF" RELIGION

The complexities and the contradictions of celebrity culture may sug- gest a religious parallel or analogy, but if this parallel is to have any force, it will need to account for both the similarities and the dissimi- larities between religion and celebrity worship. Celebrities attract a certain symbolic significance. This significance is religious or even sacred. Yet at the same time few fans (except the most extreme) appear to regard a celebrity as some kind of divine being. So if there may be a kind of sacred that belongs to some celebrities, it is manifest in rather profane and mundane flesh and blood. Similarly, when it comes to the way that celebrity worship may or may not operate as a focus for iden- tification, the religious parallels are there, but they do not line up in any unambiguous way. Clearly, some celebrities are very important to some people. Celebrities may function as images or paradigms of the possible. As such they may be regarded almost as religious figures in that that they present ideal forms of the self. They are at times sources for personal transformation and aspiration, and like religious figures they may form part of our constructed imaginary worlds. In this sense celebrities may be read as a kind of displaced religious pantheon, and yet celebrity worship is rarely if ever serious or weighty enough to be seen as any kind of ethical or even moral system. Celebrities may hint at the moral or the ethical or the aspirational, but even as they do so, few of us are far from a snigger. If celebrities are saints, then they are saints who we know have fallen, or will eventually fall, from grace. If they are gods in human form, then they not only have clay feet, they have also misplaced their underwear.

Similar observations can be made concerning the variety of prac- tices and social relationships that accompany celebrity worship. While there may be some elements of celebrity culture that appear to operate as substitute or displaced religious ritual, even those individuals most closely involved would be keen to deny that what they are engaged in is "religious." These kinds of denials may well arise from a particular understanding of what is or what is not religion, but they also serve as a corrective to the tendency for cultural commentators to use the religious analogy to explain celebrity worship. Here again celebrity culture does not appear to be able to be a religious tradition with a community and a cult as such. Yet at the same time, there are aspects of our relationships with celebrities that seem to verge upon the sacred, and this gives rise to religion-like behaviors and practices. So celebrity worship is a kind of religion, but it is a kind of religion that is not very religious.

The idea of the para-social may offer a potential vocabulary for the religious nature of celebrity culture. Perhaps it is possible to express the ambiguous relationship between celebrity culture and religion by using a phrase like "para-religion," which refers to the limited religious nature of celebrity worship. Just as para-social interactions refer to the way that celebrity worship may be relationally significant even in the absence of a face-to-face personal connection, the para-religious may offer a way to approach the partial religious significance of celebrities. Para-religion and its similarities to and differences from religious theories will be discussed in detail in chapter 3. Before this, however, celebrity worship must be situated in the context of how popular culture shapes and generates meaning and in particular how celebrities are part of a system of media-generated representation. This forms the subject of the next chapter.

2

REPRESENTATION

The quick-witted TV host introduces his show with a topical gag: "Global Warming is now on all our minds. Even the stars have realised that they must make changes to their lifestyles. Madonna has promised that she will now only fly to Africa once a year to buy a baby."[1] Cruel it may be, but it raises a smile and the audience laughs. The joke works because we know something about Madonna. It is not just that we are aware of the debate triggered by her adoption of the Malawian "orphan" David Banda—the joke is pleasurable because it touches on Madonna's celebrity "story." We know this story, and we understand that Madonna wants to be seen as doing the right thing, but we are also very well aware that she has one or two control issues. The joke works because it plays on the fact that we know, and knowing and being known are what celebrity culture is all about. There are two sides to "being known." We know about celebrities such as Madonna because they are constantly in the media. It is hard to escape knowing. Yet there is another side to knowing, where audiences are active in generating meanings around celebrities and the stories and images that represent them in the media. These two kinds of knowing form part of the discourse or communicative flow of popular culture.

Representing "the Boss"

Representation refers to the idea that what is communicated within media discourse is not so much the particular images of celebrities but the meanings that become attached to celebrities. So Bruce Springsteen, for instance, represents a kind of workingman's authenticity, just as Sandra Bullock seems to have become an icon of the Palin-esque down-to-earth "hockey mum." These meanings arise not simply from who the celebrities are but from the way media industries package and present celebrities. Their images are made up of associations. These associations or articulations, however, are not imposed on the audience by an all-powerful media. Bruce Springsteen and Sandra Bullock are made "meaningful" by the way that audiences attach meaning to them. This means that there is a form of communication or interrelationship between stars, media industry processes, and the meaning making of audiences.

Celebrities such as Bruce Springsteen "mean" different things to different people. Understanding popular culture is therefore a process of identifying how these meanings are generated and communicated. Stuart Hall, one of the key figures in the development of the academic field of cultural studies, suggests that popular culture is not so much about particular texts or commodities or things (and I would add celebrities) but about the meanings that are associated with these commodities.[2] One way to illustrate this is to talk about a single pop song. Springsteen's "Born in the USA" as a "text" can be interpreted as questioning the military policy of America. For some Republicans, however, it became a kind of nationalistic anthem. The song itself has this kind of ambiguity within its text. The verses tell of the experience of young people in war and the tragedies that come from this, but the chorus has an anthemic and slightly aggressive tone. In the U.K., Springsteen's image of the blue-jeaned American punching his fist in the air and singing "Born in the USA" was often read as American triumphalism. So "the Boss" represents a complex and contradictory symbolism. Politicians in the U.S. have courted Springsteen because he has an aura of authenticity and blue-collar decency. In the U.K. there is an undercurrent of unease about his all-American image that is tempered by the fact that he is a great songwriter, a tireless entertainer, and a survivor.

Hall says that "culture" is not located in novels or paintings, rather it is to be seen in practices. These practices, he says, are concerned with the production and communication of shared meanings within society and between groups. Springsteen as celebrity has been generated by the music industry. A range of processes and practices together make the Boss what he is. These include songwriting, performing, recording, advertising, and making videos but also include listening, going to concerts, dancing, and putting posters on your wall. These kinds of practices make up popular culture, and they enable the generation and the circulation of meanings. Culture, however, is not unitary; rather, meaning is diverse and varied.[3] People give meaning to objects and events, and over time and between cultures meanings differ in what Hall terms their "codes."[4] So "things 'in themselves' rarely if ever have any one, single, fixed and unchanging meaning."[5] This is why with an artist like Springsteen we see shifting patterns of meaning and possible interpretations. People want him to represent different things. Springsteen is interesting because he has made a kind of virtue of consistency, playing with the E Street Band throughout his career and hardly ever changing his image. He is quite different from Madonna or David Bowie, who have built their careers on the ability to morph from one image to anther. Yet even solid, reliable Springsteen has been the source of conflicting identifications.

Fifty thousand people crowded into London's Hyde Park in June 2009 to see Bruce Springsteen and the E Street Band. The band played for three hours and kicked off the show with a cover version of The Clash song "London Calling."[6] It was a symbolic gesture, even if they did rather murder the song. The symbolism of Bruce singing The Clash operates at a number of different levels: rock legend plays punk anthem, American icon identifies himself with British pop culture, New Jersey boy salutes London. All of this only makes sense because rock is a kind of "language" or a form of symbolic communication. You don't get it if you don't know the song and its background. According to Hall, popular culture is made up of meanings that are transmitted in practices, but meaning has to be shared it if is to be communicated, and those who share a culture participate in shared understandings. Through these shared images, concepts, and emotions, members of a culture "interpret

the world in roughly similar ways."[7] To communicate these shared
meanings, they must in turn share in "linguistic codes."[8] Codes combine
systems of language, and of concepts, in relation to things.[9] So popular
culture consists of systems of representation, and these work in a similar
way to a language. The rock gig is a microcosm of this "shared" language with its various codes. The fifty thousand fans in London's Hyde
Park were experiencing an event, but as they did so, and in fact in order
that they could "share" in what it meant, they needed to be able to understand the language of "rock." You don't "get" the Boss just by watching
the show. You need to be to some extent part of the culture of communication. Hall says, for instance, that the meanings of a facial gesture,
of media-generated images, of clothing, and of musical sounds do not
lie in themselves but in how they function in a system of communicat-
ing meaning.[10] Systems in turn operate in relation to wider discourses.
Celebrity culture operates as a particular kind of communication within
popular culture. So Bruce playing Hyde Park connects pop music and
the song "London Calling" with a whole range of meanings that are
associated with nationalism, location, and place.

Celebrity culture operates as flow of representation, which functions as a kind of language or a system of communication. The communicative flow of "meaning" that takes place in relation to particular
celebrities has energy and significance in popular culture because individuals find in it a source for identity. Celebrity worship is fundamentally related to the way that particular celebrities seem to attract a kind
of regard or attention. A vital element in this is the way that celebrities
such as Springsteen represent a "persona" or an image that invites identification. An interesting example of this is Springsteen's performance
of the Woody Guthrie song "This Land Is Your Land." Springsteen first
recorded the song in 1980, and he has performed it on numerous occasions. On his Born in the USA Tour in Los Angeles, he introduced the
song by saying,

> [It's] the greatest song ever written about America . . . and what's so
> great about it is it gets right to the heart of the promise of what our
> country was supposed to be about. And I guess . . . I don't know,
> if you talk to some of the unemployed steelworkers from East L.A.

or Pittsburgh or Gary, there are a lot of people out there whose jobs are disappearing. I don't know if they'd feel if this song is true any-more . . . I'm not sure that it is, but I know that it ought to be. So, I'd like to do this for you reminding you that with countries, just like with people, it's easy to let the best of yourself slip away.[11]

With this, Springsteen positions himself in relation to a particular narra-tive of American political singers that stretches from Leadbelly through Woody Guthrie and on to Bob Dylan. Yet this self-conscious "represen-tation" in turn becomes a place for the audience to form attachments and their own sense of self. In fact, Springsteen explicitly invites this kind of connection.

What Springsteen does through music, films stars do through image and narrative and supermodels do through fashion. Representation trades in images that carry multiple associations. These invite identity affiliation. The regard that makes up celebrity worship has its roots in a connection of the self to the celebrity as a source for identity. It is, however, important not to overstate the connection between celebrity and individual identity. How identity is formed in relation to represen-tation in popular culture is complicated. Hall is clear that questions of identity are complex and multilayered. They are a negotiation between subjectivity, or our sense of self, and the representation in popular cul-ture.[12] Identity, says Hall, "seems to be in the attempt to rearticulate the relationship between subjects and discursive practices that the ques-tion of identity recurs."[13] In other words, identity appears to be formed or negotiated in relation to the communicative flow of popular culture, but this is an indirect and loosely framed kind of relationship. As Hall puts it, "identities are thus points of temporary attachment to the sub-ject positions which discursive practices construct for us. They are the result of a successful articulation or 'chaining' of the subject in the flow of discourse."[14]

The idea of chaining or articulation brings together two ideas. The first relates to the way that popular culture appears to position the indi-vidual consumer. In celebrity culture this kind of positioning is seen, for instance, in the way that magazines seem to construct the reader as someone who aspires to celebrity style or, alternatively and often simultaneously, as someone who "knowingly" can spot the cellulite on the starlet's thigh or the wrinkles on her face. Hall uses the notion of "interpellation" to identify the way discourse positions and calls us.[15] Springsteen's Los Angeles introduction to "This Land Is Your Land" was an overt attempt to position his audience in relation to a particular understanding of American politics. At the same time, popular culture does not control the way that individuals make use of this kind of "call" to identification. So Hall argues that people construct their identities in relation to this kind of representation in ways that do not preclude subjectivity and agency. The audience members at Bruce's concert do not morph into an unthinking politicized group. They are free to choose the extent to which they buy into Bruce's version of what it means to be American. The flow of media-generated celebrity images and stories does not control how individual fans may or may not make use of these images and stories. Hall calls this the "production of the self."[16] Identity concerns the complex way in which individuals "produce themselves" in relation to the flow of representation in popular culture.

BEING KNOWN AS MADONNA

How we know about Springsteen, or any other celebrity for that matter, is relatively straightforward. Celebrity news makes up a huge proportion of the media output, so it is hard to escape knowing. Madonna was one of the first celebrities to grasp that the relationship between media and fame had changed. She blurred the distinction between private and public in a series of increasingly revealing projects. In 1991 she released a "fly-on-the-wall"–style documentary not only taking viewers behind the scenes of her concert tour but also allowing them to witness highly personal encounters with her family. In Europe the movie was released tellingly as *In Bed with Madonna*. The following year, her book *Sex* showed Madonna in a series of naked and some would say semipornographic poses.[17] However, according to Ellis Cashmore, it is a mistake to assume that Madonna was somehow the victim of press intrusion: "The world didn't so much 'demand' details or 'invade' her private life: they were inescapably, unavoidably, obligatorily surrounded by a life which might have been 'private' in one sense, but was open for inspection."[18] Madonna was able to reveal herself, and I mean that in more than one sense of the word, because of the willing cooperation of the media. We know about her because it is hard not to know. Through her self-revelation she made herself the product. She commodified intimacy.

Celebrity culture revolves around knowing and being known. For Daniel Boorstin, "the celebrity is a person who is well known for their well-knownness." Celebrities are "fabricated." They are manufactured, to feed our need for "exaggerated expectations of human greatness."[19] Madonna's whole career has been characterized by the ability to take up different styles in fashion and music and use them as part of her project. Image for Madonna is something to be mixed and remixed as part of the package. Its fabrication in a sense has become foregrounded as part of the entertainment. Boorstin is critical of the process whereby celebrities become famous not so much through achievement but through the ability to create a differentiation between their personality and that of others, so that while "heroes" are identified by their deeds, the celebrity is characterized through the "trivia of personality." Entertainers, he argues, are those who are most likely to be differentiated by individual personality, and they typify what he sees as the inauthentic nature of American society. Boorstin locates the source of this lack of authenticity in the way that media construct "pseudo events." A pseudo-event is one which has been created and staged solely for and by the media. Celebrities are the human equivalent of the pseudo-event, because they are a personality that has also been created solely for and by the media.[20] Celebrities are fabricated people, and in American society these artificial figures, he argues, are increasingly replacing genuine heroes.[21]

Madonna is fabricated, but that is part of the fun. As each new image and video comes out, fans and critics are able to discuss how "successful" it is. Who Madonna actually is therefore starts to shift in a pattern of changing representation. This is one of the reasons why there has been such a frenzy of interest around her marriage to film director Guy Ritchie and its eventual breakup, and her adoption of two children from Malawi, not to mention her various toy boy dalliances in more recent years. These stories seem to offer a glimpse of the "real" Madonna behind the various constructions and in ways that she does not seem to be able to manipulate or control. Of course, one of the main sources of interest has been the way that the singer has "worked" on her body and how "fit" she looks for her age. This emphasis on body as image seems to suggest that Madonna has found a way to manage her image so that even the stolen photo reveals a taut bod. Chris Rojek sees celebrity as an aspect of glamour or notoriety "in the public sphere." He argues that at a crude level celebrity equals "impact on public consciousness."[22] Celebrity is, however, distinct from renown, says Rojek. There are individuals in every society who by reason of their intelligence, sporting prowess, or some other kind of quality gain a reputation and stand out from the crowd. This kind of "renown" Rojek calls reciprocal and local in scope.[23] Celebrity is different from renown in that it is translocal. Celebrity is "ubiquitous," and yet the social contact involved is limited.[24] Social distance, says Rojek, is the precondition of both celebrity and notoriety. Yet the celebrity is also and at the same time a construct of the culture industry. Celebrities, he says, are constructs that are mediated through what he terms "chains of attraction."[25] Madonna may want to control her image, but there is a sense in which she only exists in and through her image. Her image is her business. Madonna sells, however, only because her image receives attention. Yet Madonna, like every other celebrity, has to work at this. To help her in the business of being known, there is a whole army of industry operatives and functionaries. This army includes not simply her personal stylists, publicity people, and so on—it is the much broader media world that keeps Madonna in our vision and makes sure she is known. Says Rojek, "No celebrity now acquires public recognition without the assistance of cultural intermediaries who operate to stage manage celebrity presence in the eyes of the public."[26] These cultural intermediaries include "agents, publicists, marketing personnel, promoters, photographers, fitness trainers, wardrobe staff, cosmetics experts and personal assistants."[27] This varied cast of support staff is there to ensure that the celebrity is presented in the best possible light.

WHO DOES PARIS THINK SHE IS?

In May 2008 Shallon Lester, a reporter with the *New York Daily News*, joined the crowd of hopefuls who had gathered to audition for the latest reality TV show.[28] The event was staged to find suitable contestants, and of course advance publicity for, MTV's twenty-show series *Paris*

Hilton's My New BFF. "BFF" stands for "best friend forever." The show, which has subsequently run in the U.K. and has had a second series in the U.S., is based on the conceit that Paris is lonely and wants a friend to hang out with and take to parties and other celebrity appearances. The auditions were planned to identify twenty people who would compete to become Paris' new best friend. An intrepid reporter, Shallon Lester, adopts an undercover persona of a Swedish bikini waxer, and her overtly "sexy" profession and blonde good looks ensure that she is asked back for an audition. But Lester has second thoughts. Does she really want to be known for the rest of her life as that girl from the Paris Hilton show? The reality of reality shows causes her to reflect, "While I'd like to believe that Miz Hilton and I could bond over a love of giant sunglasses and tattooed rockers, the show's winner will likely be just another fleeting fancy of the heirhead, no more important than last season's Manolos."[29]

The celebrity career of Paris Hilton has been engineered with remarkable "cheek"—cheek in both senses of the word, for her rise to celebrification has been characterized by considerable chutzpah and with the exposure of a good deal of flesh. Born in New York in 1981, the eldest daughter of Richard Hilton and Kathy Richards Hilton, Paris is one of the heirs to the Hilton fortune. As well as being born wealthy, Paris also comes from a family with significant celebrity connections. Her maternal grandmother was the actress Kathy Dugan, Zsa Zsa Gabor was married to her grandfather Conrad Hilton, and she also has family connections with Elizabeth Taylor, who was married to her great-uncle Conrad Nicholson Hilton Jr.[30] Through a mixture of modeling, minor film roles, and outrageous behavior, Paris has managed to keep herself in the public eye. In 2003 an unauthorized sex tape began to circulate on the Internet. The video showed Paris sharing intimate moments with her then-boyfriend, Rick Salomon. Salomon subsequently marketed the film under the title *One Night in Paris*, and the sales were reported to have earned him millions.[31] Despite legal proceedings against Salomon, Paris is reported to have earned a significant figure from the release of the tape, and it is often noted that the publicity generated by her sexual exploits did no harm to her first reality TV venture with the FOX network in the U.S. show *The Simple Life.*[32] As a result, thirteen million viewers tuned in to watch the premiere of *The Simple Life* and were treated to the antics of Hilton and her then–best friend Nicole Richie, who were temporarily living the rural idyll on an Arkansas farm.

Paris Hilton's rise into public consciousness illustrates the nature of contemporary celebrity culture. Rojek divides celebrity into three different kinds: ascribed, achieved, and attributed.[33] Ascribed celebrity relates to birth and family status. This form of celebrity, he says, is characterized by bloodlines in monarchy or political dynasties. So the Kennedy family, for instance, or Princes William and Harry, have a lineage, which gives them an ascribed form of celebrity. Ascribed celebrity is the reason that "kings and queens in earlier social formations commanded automatic respect and veneration. Individuals may add to or subtract from their ascribed status by virtue of their voluntary actions, but the foundation of their ascribed celebrity is predetermined."[34] Achieved celebrity, by contrast, is shaped around the accomplishments of individuals. Rojek identifies a series of figures from the sporting and the artistic worlds who are celebrities through their achievements, including Brad Pitt, Damien Hirst, Michael Jordan, Darcey Bussell, David Beckham, Lennox Lewis, and Venus and Serena Williams.[35] Achieved celebrity, however, merges with attributed celebrity because those who are famous through their achievements are often taken up and celebrated by cultural intermediaries. It is through the concentration of media representation of an individual as "noteworthy or exceptional" that celebrity becomes "attributed."[36]

Media focus and high-density coverage in the absence of any achieved or ascribed status create what Rojek calls the celetoid. Celetoids, he says, "are the accessories of cultures organized around mass communications and staged authenticity."[37] Examples of the celetoid include lottery winners, one-hit wonders, stalkers, whistle-blowers, sports arena streakers, have-a-go heroes, "and the various other social types who command media attention one day and are forgotten the next."[38] Paris Hilton's celebrity appears to be almost entirely manufactured through the media. Her renown is the result of the concentrated attention of the media, and so in Rojek's typology it is clearly attributed celebrity. At the same time, however, through the celebrity connections of her family and her status as an heiress there is an element to her fame that has its origins in her birth lineage. In other words, Paris is both an example of attributed celebrity and in some sense an ascribed celebrity. Interestingly, the ascribed celebrity appears to be on the rise, with the children of the rich and famous becoming celebrities, in some cases even before they have left school. Examples of this phenomenon include Stella McCartney, Jade Jagger, and Peaches Geldof. Yet, as with Paris, each of these can also claim to some extent to have achieved her celebrity status. Stella McCartney is a talented designer, Jade Jagger is a model, and Peaches Geldof has worked as a journalist and in TV. Paris, similarly, has generated a wide portfolio of media-related activities, including acting, singing, and TV work as well as modeling. Yet probably most important has been the way that Paris has managed to generate and sustain her media persona and find ways to exploit this financially. The ability to foster a successful celebrity persona is actually an accomplishment; in fact, one might say for Paris this is her most significant accomplishment. So Paris Hilton is also an example of achieved celebrity.

The example of Paris Hilton might suggest that Rojek's types of celebrity appear to merge when individual celebrities are under consideration. Cashmore is critical of Rojek's proposal that there are different forms of celebrity, suggesting that in practice there is no real distinction between achieved and attributed forms of celebrity: "Athletes, rock stars, models, actors, and a miscellany of celebrity lawyers, chefs, writers and so on are not just known for their knownness. The source of their renown is their prowess."[39] It is once they have become known for their achievements that cultural intermediaries take over and begin to celebrate their achievements as in some way "remarkable." Soon interest is sparked not simply in their abilities as a musician, or as a cook, or as a sports person, but also in their personal lives and relationships.[40] Just as achieved and attributed celebrity appear to merge in practice, as we have seen, the same can be said for ascribed celebrity as celebrity children become the focus of attention in the media. It is the media that above all shape the forms of celebrity. So all celebrity is, in a sense, achieved, ascribed, and attributed. As Cashmore says, "Now the distinction between ascribed, attributed and achieved celebrity has not so much blurred as erased."[41] Even royalty are in the public gaze because of the actions of the media, and so in some sense their renown is also attributed. At the same time, no one receives the attention of the media without doing something. Even if the only thing that a person has done is to appear on a reality show; and as Shallon Lester's account of auditioning for *Paris Hilton's My New BFF* demonstrates, this might also be regarded as something of an achievement.

INSIDE HOLLYWOOD—CONSTRUCTING CELEBRITY

Celebrity culture is a media-generated construct. It is the culture industry that takes ascribed and achieved celebrity and transforms it into its mediated and attributed forms. Central to these actions is the way that the media act to represent individuals as celebrities. With extensive interviews with those involved in publicity and in the Hollywood media machine, Joshua Gamson's research reveals how the industry generates renown. He describes how one of the editors of *People* magazine was clear that there was a commercial interest in the creation of celebrities: "We are a magazine that has a vested interest in to some extent creating celebrities, because these are the people you're going to get stories out of. It's about money. You need people who can sell the magazine."[42] Celebrity images sell the magazine, but the real fuel that drives the market is the stories that are spun around celebrities. The magazines trade in the stories. It is the stories that sell. Mark Frith, the editor of *Heat* magazine, shares a similar view of the importance of the story for his magazine.

In his book *Celeb Diaries*, Frith gives an intimate account of the way that celebrity stories shaped *Heat* magazine. On one occasion he speaks about the effect that the first screening of the reality TV show *Big Brother* had on his gossip-obsessed editorial team. Two of the contestants had been shown kissing on screen: "The snog. The snog! The office can talk about nothing but the snog. They're obsessed. In the middle of the office Clara and her picture team are in full swing . . . 'She's just playing with him! He's putty in her hands.' 'Rubbish, she's just playing it cool because the camera's are on her.' 'We'll see—it won't last two minutes outside, betcha.'"[43] Frith says it was then that he realized that if his editorial team in office was so caught up in this TV show then everyone else in the country must also be. Here was an opportunity for his magazine, but it was more than that, because the reality show for the first time seemed to make accessible moments and events that were generally closed to celebrity magazines. Frith explains that in the normal run of things the media are not there when a star falls in love or decides to break up with someone, but here in this show suddenly these kinds of moments were laid bare. He realized that this was the way forward for his magazine. "*Heat*, I have decided, should be like this. We should be there at the most important moments of a celebrity's life: when they fall in love (or lust), split up or are in despair. We should be the magazine equivalent of a reality TV show, a soap opera, but about real people who just happen to be famous."[44]

The move toward the real in the representation of celebrity has a history extending well before *Heat*. In the 1930s, says Gamson, the public were starting to become skeptical of the tightly controlled and stylized publicity that characterized the way stars were promoted in the film industry. This sense of the way that stars were represented led to what he calls the "pulling down of the expensive mask of glamour,"[45] ushering in the ordinary in the publicity industry. Audiences were invited to view the "real" personality behind the image. Gamson argues that this move was designed to reinforce the sense that the film stars were in some way special, set apart, and gifted. The narratives set out to convince the public that by seeing "behind the scenes" they would grasp how truly remarkable the celebrity actually was. He observes how "the at-home-with-the-famous 'inside story' was central to this process. The glamorous celebrity was thus sacrificed for the more 'realistic,' down-to-earth celebrity. Intimacy, bolstering belief was offered up."[46] This move toward the ordinary and the behind-the-scenes story was largely controlled by the Hollywood publicity machine. This managed revelation of the life of the stars was eventually to be overtaken by the much more uncomfortable world of the celebrity exposé and the paparazzi journalist.

DEALING IN EXPOSURE

The cozy world of measured intimacy between audiences and the star was symbolically shattered, says Cashmore, by a single picture. The picture was taken by an Italian photographer in 1962. The photographer was Marcello Geppetti, and at the time he was experimenting with a new piece of photographic equipment: the zoom lens. Geppetti's picture captured an image of Richard Burton and Elizabeth Taylor kissing onboard a yacht moored close to Rome on the Mediterranean coast.[47] While it might be considered rather mild by today's standards, at that time the image caused a worldwide uproar. Taylor and Burton had fallen in love while they were on the set for the movie *Cleopatra*. The picture of the kiss broke this story to the world. What caused the controversy was that at the time of the kiss both were married, not to each other but to different partners with whom they had children. The image, therefore, "signified an adulterous relationship."[48] Nevertheless, it was reproduced in newspapers and magazines all around the world. The couple was condemned by the Vatican, and the U.S. State Department was lobbied to revoke Burton's entry visa on the ground that his presence in the U.S. was "detrimental to the morals of the youth of our nation."[49] What this image symbolized was a change in the way that celebrities were treated by the media. Prior to the 1960s, even incredibly famous people such as Elizabeth Taylor could assume that their private lives would remain private and that what was revealed would only be that which the Hollywood publicist would deem appropriate. This photo, and others like it, heralded the shift in the relationship between celebrities and the media that would eventually lead to publications such as *Heat*, *People*, and the *National Enquirer*.

Frith's *Celeb Diaries* reveals how the contemporary media deal in revelation and exposure. As the book cover says, this is the "sensational inside story of the celebrity decade."[50] The book shows how access to celebrities is often highly controlled by publicity agents; so as the editor, Frith sees his job as a kind of game in which he is trying to get the better of these gatekeepers. Access may not be the only problem—he also has to try to negotiate the way that celebrities, and their agents, want to use him to present themselves in a particular light. He is always looking for the new angle, for the story that exposes and of course entertains. Yet he is not the only one who is after these stories; he is all the time competing with the daily newspapers and other magazines. *Big Brother* and the other reality shows answered Frith's need for a constant supply of new faces and accessible material. As he says in his diary entry for August 2000, "Anyone is now a celebrity. We've been the first to realise this and it's something that's helping us immensely. No one else has picked up on it . . . *Big Brother* is where we can make ourselves stand out from the competition. And rather brilliantly, there's an endless supply of new faces for us to cover too. It could have been invented for us."[51]

The representation of celebrities in the media is a negotiation between interests. On the one hand, those who are acting on behalf of the celebrity need the collaboration of their counterparts in the media; meanwhile, editors such as Frith are always searching for a story, which in many cases will be something that the celebrity does not want to reveal. These kinds of tensions are balanced by the need that celebrities and the media have of one another. They are mutually dependent.[52] As Gamson says, "The obvious shared interest in attracting consumers via celebrities is the most general basis for connections between the various subindustries. In particular, the representation and publicity industries are tightly linked both to each other (to produce and sell celebrities) and to the entertainment and entertainment-news industries (who buy and distribute their products)."[53] So those who represent celebrities and those who work to publicize them actually depend on each other. As Gamson says, "both the publicist and the journalistic organization share this fundamental commercial interest in the creation and use of brand-name celebrities for consumption."[54] Yet at the same time there is a high level of common interest, and indeed social and business communication, between those in the culture industry. Like Frith, those interviewed by Gamson most often speak about their work by using terms such as "battles" or "bargaining."[55] In these relationships, "intense mutual hostility coexists with intense mutual buttering up."[56] These different interests appear to compete and to pull in different directions, but Gamson argues that this is a vital aspect of the creative force that constructs celebrity representation. The celebrity industry is therefore one in which constant battles take place. There is a war in the "economy of information." This war centers around small pieces of personal information concerning celebrities. Says Gamson, "Bits of personality information, either written, spoken, or photographed, are the primary currency circulating and fought over between those seeking exposure and those providing it. The celebrity is divided up into pieces and these pieces move between parties, are exchanged, invested, cashed in. Each party wants in some sense to establish usage and ownership rights over the celebrities, their images and information."[57]

REPRESENTATION AND THE AUDIENCE

As we have established, celebrities are created through the processes of representation that make up the media industry. Celebrities are "well-known" because the media represent them as such. But representation is not simply a one-way process. To be well known, the image of the celebrity must gain some purchase in the imagination of the audience. For a celebrity to be "known," he or she must "mean" something. So figures such as Bruce Springsteen, Madonna, and Paris Hilton are not simply well-known for their well-knownness. Paris is "known" because she has come to represent something. Her celebrity profile appears to translate into a particular kind of influence. An example of this is that despite her sex tape and her subsequent prison stay for violating the terms of her probation for driving while under the influence of alcohol, in 2008 Paris Hilton was voted by Australian girls as one of the world's top celebrity role models.[58] For these girls Paris represented something significant about being a young woman in contemporary society. She is sassy, attractive, and successful. Paris encapsulates a certain kind of aspiration for young women, and as such she is a role model, even though she appears at times to be troubled and even though her image is clearly manufactured and marketed.

The film critic Richard Dyer argues that our fascination with celebrities arises not so much from who they are or indeed what they may have achieved but by what they represent: "Stars articulate what it is to be a human in contemporary society; that is they express the particular notion we hold of the person, of the individual."[59] Stars, Dyer says, are not simple representations of human individualism; rather, they show a glimpse of the complexity and contradictory nature of individuality. Stars "articulate both the promise and the difficulty that the notion of individuality presents for all of us who live by it."[60] The "star" is constructed from the sum of his or her media-produced images, from the roles he or she plays, and also from his or her "real"-life persona. These images are generally complex and contradictory, but they hold our interest, says Dyer, because they show us ways of living in contemporary society.[61] We are fascinated by stars because they enact different ways of "being a person" in late capitalism.[62] "Stars represent typical ways of behaving, feeling and thinking in contemporary society, ways that have been socially, culturally, historically constructed,"[63] he says. The stars are "embodiments of social categories" including gender, race, class, ethnicity, sexual orientation, and religion. The complex and contradictory images represented by celebrities are significant because they show how these constructions, at the level of the individual, are fragile and under negotiation in relation to the great social whole.[64] So for Dyer stars embody both the ordinary and the extraordinary: "They act out aspects of life that matter to us."[65]

Through the processes of representation and the ways in which these images are received and made use of by individuals, celebrity culture generates a discourse that takes us into the interplay between "identity, individuality, value and norms within cultures."[66] Celebrities are "meaningful" because it is through their representation that individuals in the wider society find cues for how to shape their own sense of self. This may be simply how to do their hair. Examples of this include the way that Farrah Fawcett's "flick" and Kevin Costner's hairstyle in the film The Bodyguard were widely imitated. This kind of imitation, David Marshall says, extended well beyond "fans" of these stars, with the hairstyles becoming a part of popular taste. The impact that celebrities have on the popularity of particular styles and items of clothing means that celebrities are often courted by the fashion industry. The industry is very well aware that the choices made by celebrities such as Will Smith, Jennifer Lopez, or Victoria and David Beckham concerning their clothes and various accessories can have a direct impact on sales. These styles may not have their origin with the celebrity, but it is the styles' "appropriation," says Marshall, which enables them to shift from high-end haute couture into popular consumption.[67] So Russell Crowe wearing a sarong and Mariah Carey opting for low-slung hip-hugger jeans both had an impact on how people chose to dress, and Madonna's adoption of underwear as outerwear, Marshall says, is the "quintessential regularisation" of a fashion style into wider popular acceptance.[68]

As they make choices, celebrities represent possible choices for the wider public. Marshall argues that "as celebrities perform individuality in their various guises, they are expressions of hyper-versions of possible transformations that anyone in consumer culture could achieve."[69] So at the same time as they are marketing things, celebrities also represent possibilities and aspirations to the consumer.[70] "We see the clothes they wear," says Cashmore, "the cars they drive and the houses they own and we want to be like them."[71] Through celebrities, shopping is transformed. It becomes a glamorous world of possibilities where celebrity style offers not only an example but, through purchases, the possibility of some kind of "identification."[72] Consumption brings a connection to or an alignment with the celebrity.

Identification between consumer and celebrity is enacted through buying products promoted by the celebrity or by adopting the style of the celebrity. These relationships are dictated not simply through the influence of advertisers and the culture industry—they are also shaped by the consumer's own life choices. Such a relationship is a "self defining relationship with the person."[73] These kinds of consumer-oriented relationships are based not so much on who consumers see themselves to be but rather on what they aspire to become. This idea has been termed the "new consumption." As explained in Cashmore's *Celebrity/Culture*, "New consumers are really seeking to discover themselves. Not the people they feel themselves to be at this moment, but the kind of men and women they aspire to be and feel it within their power to become."[74] There are degrees of identification, just as there are levels of worship, in celebrity culture. For committed fans, the identification with a celebrity may be a key element in their sense of themselves. Yet even for the average consumer there is often a level of connection at play in ordinary, everyday transactions.[75] Buying a particular product does not necessarily imply that we have developed the kind of close identification with a celebrity in the way, for instance, that extreme Elvis fans exhibit, but it may very well mean that when we buy a celebrity-endorsed product we involve in a social practice that is similar in nature if not in degree.[76] Shopping engages us in "actively shaping the self," says Cashmore. Celebrities, he continues, "have become resources when we think about ourselves, position ourselves and reflect on how we would like others to see us."[77] Celebrities are "developed to make money," but at the same time they offer us an image of ourselves or selves that we might possibly become.[78]

Celebrity culture relates directly to questions of identity and the complex interaction between media representations and the way that these influence and are taken into individual and communal senses of the self. Celebrities represent a range of possible "subject positions"; that is, they show different possibilities for individuality. The media carry these representations in the communicative practices of the entertainment industries. These representations of celebrities are "meaningful" because they offer a range of possible visions of the self. Celebrity culture therefore forms an important part of the more general flow of representation in popular culture. This flow presents possible places for identification and the development of identity: identities that are generated in relation to the flow of representation in the media.

REPRESENTATION AND WORSHIP

Identification with celebrity is one of the fundamental aspects of the "cult of the stars."[79] It is the nature of media representation that shapes identification. A key aspect of celebrity culture relates to the actual nature of the image. We do not view real people when we relate to celebrities; instead we are fixed on two-dimensional images. Cashmore likens these images to a continually moving and changing pageant. In celebrity culture the procession of figures never stops. This moving spectacle "represents for us both what we are and what (and where) we long to be."[80] John Frow also sees the actual nature of the image as being of key significance. Elvis' image, Frow says, replicates the facial features of neolithic deities. The image portrays the intensified gaze of a god. This gaze is reproduced and made into a mass-market phenomenon through the culture industry. Thus through his recordings and the continual reproduction of his image, Elvis achieves a kind of omnipresence. Technologies of reproduction place the star in place that is outside ordinary time. As a result, says Frow, "the core of stardom is thus a semiotic order. The star belongs to the domain constructed by recording and the modes of repetition specific to it which exist outside or beyond ordinary life, profane time; this is the basis for the promise that in identifying with the star, we too will overcome death."[81] For Frow, then, the image as it is repeated offers a vision of a possible sacred order.

Celebrity culture is made up of a flow of representation. The flow carries images of the possible and of the aspirational. Behind these images is an ever-developing round of narratives and stories concerning the "personal" lives of the celebrity figures. The images and the stories together offer a framework of reference and identification. It is identification that invests the celebrities with significance. They become a mirror of the self through the attention they receive. It is this attention that appears to be significant or "sacred." Offering possibilities of the sacred self, representation in celebrity culture can be seen as a kind of ordering or meaningful shaping of the potentialities of the self. Celebrity images and stories present possibilities, ways of being human, of being individuals. Celebrity worship is shaped around identification with these possible versions of the self. This identification is an essential part of the cult. It is a "kind of" religious act. This reading of celebrity culture as a pageant of sacred characters who reflect ourselves and thereby shape the possibilities of life is very similar to the American writer James Twitchell's reading of advertising as a form of religion.

In his book *Adcult USA*, Twitchell explains that advertising works by disseminating narratives. These narratives, he says, connect us to another world. For Twitchell the television commercial can be likened to a sermon or a parable, and the TV has become an altar. He describes how in the Christian religious scheme the story of salvation is peopled by a number of characters. These include the pope, the saints, bishops, priests, and nuns, all of whom are on the good side. Then representing the forces from below there are the demons, ghouls, fiends, and so on. He points out that the Christian mythic system has echoes of Greek mythological narratives, which it largely replaced.[82] Twitchell's point is that these mythical or spiritual or magical aspects of religious narratives have been taken up and relocated in the world of the advertisement. Advertisers deliberately forge links between material things (products) and the mythic. "The spirits," says Twitchell, "magically reside not in nature, holy books, magical signs, or chants but in objects as mundane as automobile tires, rolled-up tobacco leaves, meat patties, green beans, and sugar water."[83] Celebrities in a similar way appear to be invested with the "spiritual." They are significant because they are meaningful, and because they are meaningful they appear to attract notions of the "sacred."

MEANING MAKING AND RELIGION

Representation and the consumption of meanings in and through representation mean that celebrity culture is right at the heart of the process whereby the media are starting to operate in religiously significant ways. Stuart Hoover, like Chris Rojek and others, argues that changes in religious life and the media mean that there is a convergence between the two. Religion and media, Hoover says, "occupy the same spaces, serve many of the same purposes, and invigorate the same practices in late modernity."[84] So for Hoover media and religion should be thought of and theorized together rather than separately. Wade Clark Roof makes a very similar point. He sees the expansion of the media and cultural industries as having a crucial effect upon the nature and perception of religion. On one level media simply become the place where people access their information about all aspects of life, including religion. But perhaps more significantly, says Roof, the visual media serve to bolster the cultural notion of what he calls "the expansive self."[85] An expansive self, he argues, is continually in search of transcendent moments, and this search is encouraged and fed by the media. According to Roof, "the media create 'spiritual omnivores,' that is, people hungry for new experiences and insights with the hope that some encounter or revelation lying just ahead will bring greater meaning to them."[86] Religious identity involves negotiating a religious self in relation not simply to specifically religious institutions but also to the media.[87] So television, film, and other communication technologies operate in the same way as religious communities and traditions: they offer a way to structure and order life, and they present choices. The media, says Roof, are "the cultural story tellers of modern society formulating narratives of good and evil, of hope and promise, at time reinforcing at times redefining, the operative religious worlds in which people live."[88]

The media exist for economic purposes. Celebrities are there to sell things, not least themselves. The media industries are precisely that, industries. They are not religious institutions or communities. The brief glimpse into the way that the culture industry works, with its game playing, competition, and downright mendaciousness, should urge caution in listening to claims made concerning the religious significance of the media. If there are such religious overtones to celebrity culture, they operate in ways that are different from the way that formal religions operate. Media and religion may occupy the same space, but how they work must be very different. At the same time, through the "profane" activities of the media, celebrity images and stories appear to be the focus for identification. These images and stories operate as a pageant of possibilities of the self, and these possibilities together offer a way to order the world. As such there are parallels with religion, not simply because consumer culture shapes our sense of self but also because the aspirational and the meaningful in celebrities becomes a form of the "sacred." Celebrities are more then their images, more than their personal selves—they are what everyone makes of them. In this sense the celebrity becomes a reflection of what we might be, or what we might want to be, or indeed what we would hope in a million years never to be. This is what is sacred about celebrity culture. It is not the individual celebrities themselves or indeed the particular narrative of their lives— it is what people "project" onto them that is significant. So if celebrity culture is a religion or a para-religion, then at its heart is the worship of the self or the possible self. To what extent this kind of worship is or is not a religion forms the basis for the next chapter.

3

PARA-RELIGION

Celebrity worship is a kind of religion, or at least it has religious elements. Discerning the religious in popular culture is challenging, not least because religion as a generalized theoretical construct is much disputed. There are competing and contrasting ideas about the very nature of religion. The religious aspects of celebrity culture seem to resonate with many of the classic and more contemporary theories of religion that are found in anthropology, sociology, theology, and religious studies, while never really fitting any one definition. If celebrity worship is a kind of religion, then the understanding of this religion needs to be developed by drawing upon previous theoretical frameworks in an open-ended way. In a sense, an account of displaced religion in popular culture requires the displacement of theory.

Para-religion is an attempt to describe the conflicted and ambiguous religious/nonreligious nature of celebrity culture. The idea that the study of displaced religion in popular culture might require a new kind of theory of religion has been suggested by a number of scholars. Gordon Lynch, for instance, argues for a very similar approach to mediated forms of contemporary religion. Religious definition, he says, has always been a contested field with various understandings and theories in play. In this unsettled context he suggests that the study of media, religion, and popular culture can make a significant contribution to the understanding of the changing nature of religion itself.[1] Daniel Stout and Judith Buddenbaum suggest that research into religion and popular culture will necessarily involve the development of new vocabularies in religious studies.[2] Fundamental to research into popular media, they argue, are questions that address what kind of "religion" is mediated in and through popular culture.[3] This is precisely what is intended by the term "para-religion."

Religion has been widely debated and variously defined. But most definitions of religion, be they essentialist, functionalist, or phenomenological, tend to exclude celebrity worship as a formal "religion." So whatever the definition of "religion," celebrity culture seems to be outside of the theory for one reason or another. On the principle that if it looks like a dog and walks like a dog and barks like a dog then it is a dog, we might be justified in concluding that celebrity worship is not really a religion. Actually I am in considerable sympathy with this view—celebrity worship should probably not be seen as a traditional religion. The problem, however, is that various aspects of celebrity worship seem to be meaningful to people in ways that suggest a "kind of" religious parallel. This is where the idea of para-religion may be useful. Rather than dismissing celebrity worship as not religiously significant by adapting different elements from a range of theories of religion, it might be possible to cast new light on how, through the action of the media, and through the agency of audiences and fans, something like (and not like) religion is starting to emerge.

SPIRITUAL BEINGS

A classic essentialist definition of religion is the nineteenth-century anthropologist Sir Edward Tylor's notion of "belief in spiritual beings."[4] This belief he called "animism," and he argued that it forms the basis of all religious systems. Taking the term from the Greek word for soul, *anima*,[5] Tylor suggested that animism created the "groundwork" for all religion. Animism was based, however, on a distinction between a belief in souls and a belief in spirits. This belief arose, said Tylor, when "primitive peoples" began to reflect on the difference between a dead and a living body, a rational reflection which led to the idea of the soul. The concept of the spirit, on the other hand, emerged as people considered the meaning of dreams.[6] Tylor argued that the linguistic connections between ideas—for example, wind, breath, life, and shadow—have parallels in the religious concepts of soul and spirit. In preliterate cultures, he suggested, plants and animals are often regarded as having souls. The idea of the soul then developed into a belief in spiritual beings. So for Tylor religious myth concerning the soul and the spirit emerges as a form of reasoning about the world.[7] Tylor's conception of religion as belief in spiritual beings shares common elements with Herbert Spencer's understanding of the development of religion as having its origins in early people's experiences of death and dreams. In prehistory, Spencer argued, these experiences led to the conceptualization of a distinction between the body and the soul. Ghosts were central to the origins of belief in spiritual beings, and according to Spencer the ghost is "[t]he first traceable conception of a supernatural being.[8] The mythic world of divinities and gods subsequently emerged from the practice of ancestor worship, which forms the root for all religion.

The assertion that all religion has arisen from a common source or essence is now generally seen as problematic.[9] Celebrity culture, however, does carry aspects of the idea of "spiritual beings." Morin's notion of the star as a semidivine figure of worship seems to draw directly on these early anthropological treatments of religion. Morin starts his book *The Stars* with a quote from playwright George Bernard Shaw: "The savage worships idols of wood and stone; the civilised man, idols of flesh and blood."[10] Obviously Shaw's language is of its time, but the take on contemporary "idolatry" is very suggestive. If celebrity worship is a religion, then it is the worship of the human form. Celebrity worship is centered on the image and the idol, but these are representations of the human or the possibilities of what it is to be human. However, in celebrity worship the use of the terms "god" or "idol" does not refer to any kind of transcendence. Celebrities are not supernatural or spiritual beings, they do not represent a "beyond." If they are spiritual, it is only in the sense that everyone is spiritual.

MYTH AND RITUAL

Some of the early essentialist theories explored the link between myths (of spiritual beings) and the ritual practices of communities. This approach to religious definition has often been taken up by scholars and adapted in ways that account for the religious aspects of popular culture. Eric Mazur, for instance, makes a connection between contemporary religion and ideas of myth and ritual: "Myths and legends of various religious traditions resurface—by themselves, in fragments, and in strange combinations—in what look like wholly secular spaces, in a process that both keeps the stories alive and radically reframes their meaning."[11] But these traditional categories of ritual, myth, and religious institution, Mazur suggests, must be "stretched" if they are to take account of the changing nature of religion and in particular if they are to be seen as having any kind of purchase on the way that religion is interacting with popular culture. This is the "strange new world of religion in contemporary America."[12] This notion of the need to adapt, stretch theory, is helpful in approaching celebrity culture, in which there are clearly "mythic" elements and "rituals" but in which these two elements do not seem to create a religion in the way that classic essentialist theories may suggest.

For the nineteenth-century anthropologist William Robertson Smith, the essence of religion was not mythic notions of the soul but ritual. Religion, he argued, was constructed from acts of worship that reinforced communities: "Religion was made up of a series of acts and observances," and these did not exist for the sake of saving souls "but for the preservation and welfare of society."[13] Smith saw myth as being subsequent to and largely derived from ritual. Rituals were fixed and did not change, he argued, while myths were more flexible: "the myth was derived from the ritual, and not the ritual from the myth; for ritual was fixed and the myth was variable, the ritual was obligatory and faith in the myth was at the discretion of the worshipper."[14]

The narratives and images that make up celebrity culture have "mythic elements." Through the processes of representation celebrities seem to attract religious references and analogies. These mythic elements, however, are much more fluid and unfocused than essentialist theorists would expect in a formal religion. In much the same way, there are ritual elements to celebrity culture. There is the ritual of the revealing interview, or the posed photograph in the skimpy dress on the red carpet, or the picture with the wife who is sticking by you. These may be rituals, but we would be hard-pressed to see in them any coherent link to religious myth in the way that it is described by Smith. Even where celebrity culture gathers a community around the performance of a ritual—at, for instance, a sports event or a rock concert—it is quite a stretch to see in such gatherings a religion that preserves society. At the same time there do seem to be both mythic and ritual elements at play in celebrity worship. An example of this is Chris Rojek's suggestion that celebrity narratives draw upon the essentialist theory that all religion is shaped around a common mythic pattern of the god/king who dies and rises again.

The dying and rising god myth is closely associated with J. G. Frazer's classic work on religion, *The Golden Bough*, first published in 1890.[15] Frazer argued that behind all ritual was a universal pattern, which came from the ritual performance of the death and resurrection of a god or a divine king. This enacted death and resurrection ensured the well-being of the community.[16] Frazer said that "in antiquity the civilised nations of Western Asia and Egypt pictured to themselves the changes of the seasons, and particularly the annual growth and decay of vegetation as episodes in the life of gods, whose mournful death and happy resurrection they celebrated with dramatic rites of alternate lamentation and rejoicing."[17] The ritual of the dying and rising god king was not simply a feature of the religion of the East; Frazer traces it to ancient Greece and on into the religions of the West. Yet while these celebrations were dramatic, they were also in a sense magical, because they ensured the continuation of the seasons and the cycle of growth and decay that shaped agrarian life.[18]

Rojek uses Frazer's idea of the dying and rising god myth to discuss celebrity culture.[19] "Descent and falling," Rojek says, "are twinned with ascent and rising. Elevation is in itself, a source of envy as well as approval. Celebrities acquire so much honorific status and wealth that their downfall becomes a matter of public speculation and, on occasion, is even desired."[20] Media accounts of the rise and fall of celebrities such as Britney Spears, George Michael, and Amy Winehouse appear to support this reading of celebrity culture as myth. The difference is that the narratives and stories that make up celebrity culture, while they may be seen as "mythic," do not operate in relation to society in any of the ways imagined by Frazer. It is one thing to identify a mythic pattern in media accounts of celebrity; it is quite another to assert that these stories have a cosmic effect. So celebrity culture picks up on aspects of religion as they are described in the essentialist theories, but there are key elements of these theories that clearly do not apply to this aspect of popular culture in the way that they were first conceived.

RELIGION AND SOCIETY

Classic essentialist accounts of religion "sort of" fit celebrity culture, and they "sort of" don't fit. A similar pattern of a partial correlation between theory and celebrity worship is repeated with functionalist definitions of religion. The idea that celebrity worship functions like a religion, or as a substitute for religion, is actually a very common assertion both in academic and popular commentary on contemporary culture. These assertions, however, are not really supported by Emile Durkheim, the most significant source for functionalist theories of religion.

In his work *The Elementary Forms of Religious Life*, Emile Durkheim rejects essentialist definitions of religion that are focused on the supernatural or the transcendent. Religion, he argues, is not constituted by belief in gods or the spirits.[21] Instead, religion is based on the distinction between the sacred and the profane: "all known religious beliefs . . . present one common characteristic: they presuppose a classification of things, real and ideal, of which men think, into two classes or opposed groups, generally designated by . . . the words profane and sacred."[22] Religious beliefs express the sacredness of things, while religious rituals constitute the "rules of conduct," that is, how people should act when they are in the presence of sacred objects.[23] Durkheim focuses on the unifying function of religion in society: "A religion is a unified system of beliefs and practices relative to sacred things, that is to say, things set apart and forbidden—beliefs and practices which unite into one single moral community called a Church, all those who adhere to them."[24] Durkheim emphasizes the significance of the second part of this definition: religion, he says, "must be an eminently collective thing."[25] Religion is something that is held in common by a religious group. It cannot be regarded as an individual preference because belief shapes group feeling. People feel they belong to a group because they share the faith of the group.[26] In support of this assertion, says Durkheim, "In all history, we do not find a single religion without a church."[27]

Religion also functions to reinforce social bonds. Rituals, religious ceremonies, and festivals provide moments when the community may gather to experience what Durkheim calls "effervescence," a state in which "[m]an is carried outside of himself, pulled away from his ordinary occupations and preoccupations."[28] This emotional response to a ritual gathering causes the individual to identify with the larger group through an encounter with something that is larger than himself or herself.[29] At the heart of the sense of a religious identity lies the religious symbol of the totem. Totemic symbols, says Durkheim, "possess the greatest sanctity."[30] The source of religion lies not so much in these objects but in what these objects represent. Durkheim argues that the religious symbol of the totem signifies both the deity or god and also the clan to which this symbol is of particular significance. Durkheim concludes from this that if the symbolic representation of the totem refers both to a god and to society, then these two are in fact one: "Thus the god of the clan, the totemic principle, can be none other than the clan itself, but the clan transfigured and imagined in physical form of the plant or animal that serves as totem."[31] For Durkheim, then, religion is society worshipping itself.

The functionalist understanding of religion is further developed in the anthropologist Clifford Geertz' more recent work examining religion as a cultural system. Religion, he argues, is a system that shapes and affects people's senses and action through a structuring of life. Religious symbols operate as a system to form an understanding of life and to frame how that life should be lived. So religion both presents an idealized image of the order of things and at the same time brings that order into being.[32] Geertz defines religion as "(1) a system of symbols which acts to (2) establish powerful, pervasive, and long-lasting moods and motivations in men by (3) formulating conceptions of a general order of existence and (4) clothing these conceptions with such an aura of factuality that (5) the moods and motivations seem uniquely realistic."[33] The symbolic system of culture, therefore, arises as a response to questions of meaning that result from human experience. So the experiences of suffering or death give rise to systems of meaning that operate as a response to experience.[34] In religious ritual, this worldview is enacted and lived out, but it also induces an ethos or a way of motivating those who share in the religious event. So for Geertz, in a religious ritual, "the world as lived and the world as imagined, fused under the agency of a single set of symbolic forms, turn out to be the same world."[35] Religion therefore becomes a place where a group's ideals concerning the world and also the actual experience of life might influence each other. Thus religion operates to provide the means for a continual process of adaptation and renewal in communities.[36]

The common assertion that celebrity worship functions like a religion is hard to sustain. Celebrity worship falls some way short of religion as it is described in the functionalist theories typified by Durkheim and Geertz. There is no group or unified church in celebrity worship. It is difficult to see how the images and practices associated with celebrity contribute to a collective well-being or to any kind of societal order. There are, however, totemic or symbolic elements of celebrity worship. These symbols are "meaningful," but not in the wholesome ways described in functionalist theory. Celebrity worship is not society worshipping itself, as Durkheim suggested of religion, but it is a kind of self-worship. The self, however, is not a collective self but the sum of individual selves. Parallels exist between celebrity worship and the idea of religion as cultural system, but these similarities also carry significant differences. It is hard, for instance, to talk about the "seriousness" of celebrity culture as a meaningful response to issues of suffering or mortality. Suffering and mortality may be at play in celebrity worship, but they are carried in a confusing mix of the mundane, the ridiculous, and the prurient. Mazur argues that Geertz' understanding of religion as a cultural system can contribute to an understanding of the religious aspects of popular culture, but it can only do so if the definition remains "fuzzy."[37] Celebrity worship is the sacred without the moral and the totem without the social. Similarity of celebrity worship to religion, such as the appearance of celebrities in some form of sacred representation, remains analogical or metaphorical. While religious or theological themes are articulated in representation with the images of the stars, they have no predictable or necessary correspondence to any kind of religious practice or

religious community. So the symbolic is disconnected from a function-
ing religious life just as it is dislocated from any essentialist reference
point in transcendence. It is the theological floating in the circulation
of representation.

THE NUMINOUS AND THE SACRED

Representation makes gods out of mortals and idols out of stars. There
is an "apotheosis associated with the modern star system," says John
Frow, that is a phenomenon of a "strictly religious order."[38] Celebrities
such as Elvis and Diana are demigods, intercessory figures who "span
the divide between two worlds."[39] Media's reproduction of the image and
voice of the star is what creates the transformation of a mortal into the
semidivine. So for Frow, "The power that Elvis generated, that he himself sought to explain by means of astrology, numerology, and Christian
revivalist lore, had a much more mundane origin in a technology of repetition: at once the withdrawal of sound and image from the linear flow
of time, and their dissemination in an endless series of copies."[40] This
flow of media processes transforms Elvis, but this transformation takes
the form of an encounter with mystery. To explain this religious element
in perception of Elvis by his fans, Frow introduces the phenomenological category of "the holy," which he takes from the work of the German
theologian Rudolf Otto.

In *The Idea of the Holy*, Otto argues for an understanding of religion that explores the phenomenon of the individual encounter with the
sacred. Otto invites his readers to explore their own "deeply-felt religious experience," the "states of the soul" as they are encountered in
solemn worship, and to seek out "what is unique in them."[41] For Otto
what is unique in these moments is what he calls the sense of a "creature-
consciousness or creature feeling."[42] This, he says, is "the emotion of a
creature, submerged and overwhelmed by its own nothingness in contrast to that which is supreme above all creatures."[43] Creature feeling
is generated from the "shadow" of another feeling. This shadow, says
Otto, is cast by something which is "an object outside the self."[44] This
outside object is "the numinous," and for the creature feeling to arise,
the numen must be present. "There must be felt a something 'numinous,'
something bearing the character of a 'numen,' to which the mind turns

spontaneously; or (which is the same thing in other words) these feelings can only arise in the mind as accompanying emotions when the category of 'the numinous' is called into play."[45]

The experience of the numinous other is characterized by what Otto calls the *mysterium tremendum*.[46] *Mysterium* simply denotes the hiddenness of the other that remains beyond our comprehension even as it is experienced. *Tremendum*, on the other hand, is the emotion of fear. It is religious dread or awe that lies at the root of all religion.[47] In early religion, fear of ghosts and demons is revealed by a "shudder." In contemporary forms of worship, the use of phrases such as "Holy, Holy, Holy" in songs and liturgy indicate that in Christian worship *mysterium tremendum* has continuing endurance. "The 'shudder,'" says Otto, "has here lost its crazy and bewildering note, but not the ineffable something that holds the mind. It has become a mystical awe, and sets free as its accompaniment, reflected in self consciousness, that 'creature-feeling' that has already been described as the feeling of personal nothingness and submergence before the awe-inspiring object directly experienced."[48]

The idea of the holy centers on the phenomenon of an encounter with a divine other. As a theory of religion, although it is focused on the phenomenological as it is evident in experience, it is orientated toward notions of transcendence. It is hard to see how this phenomenon of an encounter with the holy can have any purchase in celebrity culture. Celebrity worship does not support of necessity any sense that there is a greater other beyond the human. In fact, it has trouble moving beyond handbags, shoes, breasts, and haircuts. Even in a reproduced form the image of Elvis does not carry any clear or necessary association with the transcendent—as many fans are at pains to make clear. Yet there remains a sense that in the celebrity something exists that is greater than that individual. The numinous is invoked by cultural commentators such as Frow as an analogy rather than as a reference to any divine encounter. As analogy or metaphor the numinous appears to be present; however, it does not connect us to a transcendent other but to the more earthbound and corporeal sense of ourselves. The other that is reflected in the star is the sum of our own aspirations. The apotheosis of the celebrity is the reflected glory of our own aspirational image. The sacred is thereby merged with the profane.

THE SACRED AND THE PROFANE

Otto's phenomenological understanding of religion as the "holy" is adapted by Mircea Eliade in his seminal text *The Sacred and the Profane*. For Eliade the sacred is revealed through "hierophany," that is, something sacred that shows itself. And the sacred, he says, is simply "the opposite of the profane."[49] The history of religion is constituted from a series of hierophanies. From the most "elementary" hierophany of the sacred in an object such as a rock or a tree to what Eliade calls the "supreme hierophany," which in the Christian faith is the coming of Christ, we are confronted by the same "mysterious act."[50] In these acts we are in the presence of what Eliade describes as "a wholly different order, a reality that does not belong to our world, in objects that are an integral part of our natural 'profane' world."[51] For the religious space, says Eliade, manifests an interruption or a break in the order of things. The religious space becomes "holy ground."[52] The hierophany demonstrates the "non homogeneity of space," and it is this kind of rupture that "allows the world to be constituted, because it reveals the fixed point, the central axis for all future orientation."[53] So in the moment of revelation we see that which is opposed to the "non reality" of the surrounding world. In the midst of the profane reality we see "absolute reality."[54]

Yet there is a paradox in every hierophany, because "[b]y manifesting the sacred, any object becomes something else, yet it continues to remain itself."[55] So a sacred stone continues to be a stone, but for those "for whom the stone reveals itself as sacred its immediate reality is transmuted into sacred reality."[56] Religious feeling is shaped around the attempt to remain as far as is possible in the sacred world as long as possible. To reject religion, however, is to live in a "de-sacralized world."[57] Eliade observes that in the "completely profane world the wholly desacralized cosmos is a recent discovery in the history of the human spirit."[58] Even in the most desacralized societies, however, Eliade suggests that the sacred may still be present: "The majority of the 'irreligious,'" he says, "still behave religiously."[59]

The suggestion that celebrity worship is a form of displaced religion has its roots in Eliade's work. Modern people, says Eliade, although they may not see themselves as particularly religious, retain "camouflaged myths and degenerated rituals."[60] Thus the mythic, Eliade argues, is disguised or hidden in the movies, novels, and plays that come out of the modern "dream factories" of the entertainment industry: "Strictly speaking, the great majority of the irreligious are not liberated from religious behaviour, from theologies and mythologies. They sometimes stagger under a whole magic-religious paraphernalia, which, however, has degenerated to the point of caricature and hence is hard to recognize for what it is."[61]

Gordon Lynch argues that a modified form of Eliade's notion of the sacred may be a potential starting point for an understanding of the changing nature of religion in media culture. But Lynch finds the duality in Eliade's thought between the sacred and the profane to be unhelpful.[62] Lynch also rejects the link between the sacred and notions of transcendence. In their place he argues for the importance of "sacred objects": "The sacred is an object defined by a particular quality of human thought, feeling and behaviour in which it is regarded as a grounding or ultimate source of power, identity, meaning and truth. This quality of human attention to the sacred object is constructed and mediated through particular social relations, and cultural practices and resources."[63] So for Lynch the sacred is made up of the particular thoughts and feelings, actions and practices that develop in relation to the sacred object. He argues that a particular "quality of response" to the sacred object, characterized by intense orientation and focus, constitutes the human relationship with the sacred. At the same time he suggests that orientation toward the sacred brings people into communal relationships and shared identities.[64]

Lynch's suggestion that the dualism of the sacred and the profane is collapsed in popular culture is very helpful. This notion describes how the religious undergoes change in celebrity representation. Lynch's understanding of the sacred as the object of a particular kind of feeling and behavior, however, does not really describe celebrity worship. This understanding of the sacred is helpful in examining particular instances of extreme fan worship, but for the vast majority of celebrity culture this kind of "regard" is largely absent. What we have instead is the merging of the sacred and the profane at the level of representation. This appropriation of the religious or the theological is dislocated from any specific religious feelings or practices. Defined in Lynch's terms, celebrity worship is not religion. In many ways celebrity worship is more akin to Eliade's original notion of the sacred that has in some way been degenerated or emptied of meaning.

CONTEMPORARY APPROACHES TO RELIGION

While the idea of celebrity culture as "kind of" religion is quite common, the classic theories, be they essentialist, functionalist, or phenomenological, do not really support this. More recent theories of religion have tended to read the new religious context in three ways: first, in the move away from a religion of the transcendent other toward a religion of the self; second, in the effect that media has had on this religious shift; and third, in the way that religion might be described from the perspective of the religious subject. Each of these contributes to an understanding of celebrity worship in significant ways. Celebrity culture in many ways is a part of this new religious terrain, in particular in the way that changes in religion are seen as having a relationship to media and popular culture and the turn to the self and the subjective. At the same time, some elements of these recent religious theories do not describe celebrity culture. Celebrity worship, even in this new theoretical terrain, is still an uncomfortable fit. These theories, however, as with the classic accounts of religion, contribute elements that might be used in describing celebrity worship as a sort of religion or as a para-religion.

Expressive Individualism

The contemporary religious environment is characterized by a shift in religious sensibility toward "expressive individualism," according to sociologist Paul Heelas. The focus on the individual, Heelas argues, leads to the collapse of differentiation. So the spirituality of "the perennial" has meant a journey from religious exclusivism to inclusivism.[65] Differentiation, which had been a characteristic of modern religious culture, leads to what Heelas terms "dedifferentiation."[66] In the dedifferentiated environment religious differences may remain, but they are no longer supported by plausible systems of rational argument or truth claims, and as a result they are "de-regulated and un-policed." What is different is now just seen as being different: "The cultural becomes

disorganized; less black and white. The distinction between the high
and the low fades way. The claim that one tradition should be adhered
to because it and it alone is valid, is rendered invalid."[67]

Questions of authority and legitimacy become the preserve of the
individual and his or her choices. This focus on individual choice has
led to the collapse of the distinction between secular and religious discourses. The individual no longer feels constrained by the boundaries of
tradition. Choice leaves the subject as an autonomous arbitrator between
sources both religious and nonreligious as they are "diffused in culture."[68] So autonomous individuals "raid the world, drawing on whatever
is felt desirable: the religious (perhaps shamanism and Christianity); the
religious and the non-religious (perhaps yoga and champagne)."[69] The
existence of this religion of choice, however, does not necessarily mean
that religious traditions collapse, says Heelas; in fact there are signs that
these traditions have been able to endure.[70] Traditions may survive, but
they undergo significant changes, a process that Heelas and coauthor
Linda Woodhead call "the subjective turn."[71]

According to Heelas and Woodhead, "the turn" is a move away
from life "lived in terms of external or objective roles, duties and obliga-
tions, and a turn towards life lived by reference to one's own subjective
experiences (relational as much as individualistic)."[72] So the subjective
turn, they argue, is a shift away from what they call "life-as" and a move
toward "subjective-life." "Life as" is characterized by a sense of duty
to perform roles as parent, wife, leader, disciple, etc., whereas "subjective-life" is framed around what the authors describe as life "lived in
deep connection with the unique experiences of my self-in-relation."[73]
Thus there is a departure from a religious environment where people
see themselves in relation to orders of life that are greater or that are
outside and transcendent.[74] Instead there is turn toward subjectivity,
where the things that matter are "states of consciousness, states of mind,
memories, emotions, passions, sensations, bodily experiences, dreams,
feelings, inner conscience, and sentiments—including moral sentiments
like compassion."

Celebrity worship reflects many aspects of the turn to self. Indeed,
celebrity culture is one way that this turn is resourced and generated in
consumer society. Wade Clark Roof describes the shift toward the indi-

vidual in religion as a move toward the "expansive self."[75] The expansive self, located in "feelings, sensitivities, expressiveness, or simply [in] individuality,"[76] positions the individual as one who explores the inner life, and the self becomes the focus of attention and energy. Developing the inner life through a process of transformation becomes part of the definition of the individual.[77] Alongside the expansive self, religion has also been shaped by a consumer culture that caters to all the casual wants and desires of American society. The consumer culture has fed the hungry selves of the baby boomer generation with a series of products made "just for them." The advertising industry has offered a steady stream of promises for a better life and constant improvement. This has wrought a change in religion so that the question "How can I be saved?" has been replaced by the question "How can I feel good about myself?"[78] If, as we have discussed, the worship of celebrity is the worship of the self writ large, then celebrity culture is a key element in the media-generated religious environment that stimulates and supports notions of the expansive self.

Media

Central to this shift toward the self in religion has been the way that the media feed the expansive self. As Roof says, "Never before has human life been so caught up in mediated image and symbol. And never before have people themselves been so aware that ours is such a world of image and symbol."[79] The media encourage the sense that people are empty and in need of filling. As such it generates a steady succession of what Roof calls "moments of transcendence."[80] The media create "spiritual omnivores" hungry for the next experience and the next revelation, and it encourages the hope that these experiences will bring greater meaning. Roof suggests that in this new marketplace of mediated religion the nature of the religious change is not fully understood, but he is clear that religion is undergoing what he calls a "considerable recasting"[81] taking place in three main ways. First is instrumentality, where religion changes in relation to how it meets the practical needs of people. Second is commodification, in which religion becomes a product offered in and through the media. Third is an adhesive process whereby symbols, images, technologies, and practices are mixed together to form a unity focused on the individual. Finally the media generate a perception of accessibility whereby the consumer has a direct access to spiritual goods. This is what Roof calls a "deregulated and de-monopolized world."[82]

Stout and Buddenbaum, like Roof, emphasize the impact of the media on religion. They use the term "mediated religion" to describe these changes. Examples of mediated religion include televangelism, religious radio, megachurches, emerging churches, religious films, and faith blogs.[83] Mediation of religious life, however, does not simply relate to the way that religious communities make use of media or how they might be portrayed in the media. There is also a growing awareness that mediation performs religious functions and can be interpreted through religious frameworks of understanding.[84] Stuart Hoover, for instance, argues that these changes in religious life in relation to the media should be seen as a kind of "convergence" of religion and the media. Religion and the media, Hoover argues, occupy the same spaces and serve the same function.[85] For Roof, a mediated consumer culture remakes religion into a "self-reflexive activity" where the individual is engaged in an active process of meaning making:[86] "Bombarded by media input, the individual is left having to do a lot of cognitive negotiating and bargaining."[87] The media, he argues, take on some of the characteristics of religion: "Television and film thus assume some of the functions traditionally assigned to religious myth and ritual. They are the cultural storytellers of modern society formulating narratives of good and evil or hope and promise, at times reinforcing, at times redefining, the operative religious worlds in which people live."[88] This religious function, however, is limited by the social connections that operate in and through media. Electronic communities, Roof points out, lack face-to-face interaction, which means that the media are restricted in their ability to sustain spiritual life and instead offer "fleeting glimpses" of reality and transcendence. At the same time the media processes of encoding and decoding leave questions of meaning to be negotiated from an overarching complexity by the individual.[89]

Roof sees promise in this mediated religious environment because it opens up spaces for the sacred; but at the same time, the symbols that the environment generates are flawed. Mediated religious content consists of "broken symbols"; these are symbols that the individual is fully aware have been humanly constructed and so are "inherently finite and limited." This does not mean that these symbols may not be places for divine encounter, but it is an encounter that always carries the rider that it is a vision, provisional and fundamentally precarious.[90] The contemporary religious landscape, according to Mazur, reveals "the changing manner in which society expresses itself religiously."[91] This has the implication, he says, that we may find meaning where "we may not otherwise have looked; in the visit to the dentist, the bathroom or the hospital. Meaning can be found in the 'meaningless.'"[92] Mazur describes his account of religion in popular culture as a kind of mapmaking that focuses on the borderland where popular culture and religion meet. This is a borderland where the traditional language of religion may not be used but its accent can still be discerned.[93]

Authentic Fakes

The idea of broken symbols is echoed in David Chidester's notion of "fake religion." American popular culture is characterized by inauthentic religion, argues Chidester. Baseball, rock and roll, and Coca-Cola attract to themselves some of the characteristics of religion and "pose" as religion relocated in popular culture. For instance, baseball is often spoken of by its fans as a kind of church: "The 'Church of Baseball' involves much more than merely a rule book. It is a religious institution that maintains the continuity, uniformity, sacred space, and sacred time of American life. As the 'faith of fifty million people,' baseball does everything that we conventionally understand to be done by the institution of the Church."[94] In a very similar way, Coca-Cola, says Chidester, has taken on the characteristics of a sacred object. It is a fetish, an object with a "sacred aura."[95] Coca-Cola supplied the West with one of its most significant religious figures, Father Christmas. By the 1930s Coca-Cola had become a symbol of the "sublimated essence of America."[96] Rock and Roll, says Chidester, is characterized by a communcal sharing or potlatch. This carries within it a kind of religious essentialism.[97]

Baseball, Coca-Cola, and rock and roll are not religion, yet they seem to take on the appearance of religion and as such develop strange forms that in themselves question how religion might be understood. According to Chidester, baseball, Coca-Cola, and rock and roll are "re-familiarised as if they were religion."[98] In this way Chidester seems to blur the boundaries between traditional definitions of what constitutes religion and how religious elements may be taken up and dislocated in the discourses of popular culture. This blurring of the boundaries is in part what the idea of para-religion is trying to address. Celebrity culture is part of what Chidester describes as an authentic fake. Celebrity manifests the way that echoes of the "transcendent" persist as "traces" in popular culture.[99]

Religion as a Chain of Memory

The idea that there may some kind of religious analogy or metaphor that is operating in culture is a key point of departure for the French sociologist Danièle Hervieu-Léger. She draws upon the work of J. Seguy, who identifies the idea of the "metaphorical" use of religion in the work of Max Weber. Thus in Weber's thinking the political struggles in Europe can be likened the battles of the gods on Olympus. The polytheism of political allegiance gives rise to beliefs, acts of devotion and sacrifice, and the experience of ecstasy. "We describe this religion as analogical," says Seguy, "because it does not refer to supernatural powers, but possesses most of the other features of religion in the full sense of the term."[100] This kind of metaphorization is a result of modernity, and it takes place not only in secular or profane traditions but also in formal religious traditions, where aspects of transcendence become "spiritualized."

Hervieu-Léger builds on this theory to posit the notion that religion is situated in the passing on of tradition as a way of believing. She argues for an understanding of belief that empties it of both its content and its function and suggests that believing depends upon belief's legitimation as part of an ongoing tradition.[101] So, Hervieu-Léger argues, "one would describe any form of believing as religious which sees its commitment to a chain of belief it adopts as all-absorbing."[102] She then uses this definition of religion to assess the appearance of religion in sports. Hervieu-Léger makes a distinction between the possibility of the sacred in sporting events (or indeed rock concerts or any other mass rituals) and religion as the participation in a chain of memory: "What ritual occasions in sport display in their very immediacy is in fact the dissociation, characteristic of modern societies, between sacredness (as collective experience of the presence of a force transcending individual consciousness and hence producing meaning) and religion (as ritualized remembering of a core lineage, in relation to which present experience constructs meaning)."[103] Spectator sports and other aspects of popular culture such as telethons and rock concerts "offer in small pieces . . . access to an experience of the sacred (an immediate, emotional realization of meaning) which en masse no longer functions in the religious mode."[104] For Hervieu-Léger popular culture offers a form of the sacred, but this is not religion, because it is disconnected from the chain of meaning in a tradition. It is precisely this kind of disconnect that is seen in elements of celebrity culture.

Lived Religion

Meredith McGuire suggests in her book *Lived Religion* that an examination of people's religious lives challenges the understandings of religion orientated around "affiliation or institutional participation.[105] She argues that scholars should no longer view religion as "some kind of trans-historical essence, existing as a timeless and unitary phenomenon,"[106] suggesting that the focus should not be so much on universal definitions of religion but upon the study of individuals as they practice religion. This leads McGuire to view "religion" as something that changes over time as the individual constructs and reconstructs his or her sense of self in relation to religious texts and institutions. "At the level of the individual, religion is not fixed, unitary, or even coherent." We should expect that all person vs' religious practices and the stories with which they make sense of their lives are always changing, adapting, and growing. Individual religion, however, is also social. The individual constructs meaning from the "building blocks" made available in religious communities. These include shared meanings, learned practices, borrowed imagery, and imparted insights. According to Robert Orsi, religion should be seen as "the practice of making the invisible visible, of concretizing the order of the universe, the nature of human life and its destiny, and the various dimensions and possibilities of human interiority itself, as these are understood in various cultures at different times, in order to render them visible and tangible, present to the senses in the circumstances of everyday life."[107] Religious rituals therefore make a world in which people can dwell.[108]

The lived religion of the Elvis fan, as we have seen, is a contested field. Doss is clear that many fans would dispute that their relationship to the King is religious at all.[109] Yet at the same time she identifies the practices and the rituals she observed in Elvis fans as a form of religion. Doss argues that religion and religious attitudes run deep in American culture: "As a profoundly religious people, Americans tend to treat things on religious terms, apply religious categories, and generally make a religion out of much that is touched and understood."[110] Americans are inclined to mix and match their religious beliefs and practices, drawing upon a range of sources. So the objection to the idea that Elvis fans' practices are religious, Doss suggests, might well be drawn from a more narrow understanding of religion than that which she is using in her research. For Doss, religion is constituted by "practices and attitudes that imbue a person's life with meaning by linking him or her to a transcendent reality; that which is beyond purely immanent, or secular, experience and understanding."[111] So for Doss the varieties of practices and rituals associated with Graceland and the way that many fans create sacred spaces in their homes reserved for Elvis are an indication that for some being a fan involves a form of belief.[112]

"THEOLOGY" AND POPULAR CULTURE

Contemporary theories of religion offer a range of ways of approaching and understanding celebrity culture. The interaction between representation and identification in celebrity worship accords well with key themes from religious studies and the sociology of religion. The ideas of subjectivity and the turn toward the self describe significant elements of celebrity worship. The identification of the importance of media and popular culture for the changing nature of religion clearly situates celebrity culture within these theoretical frameworks. In addition to this is the question of the form in which the religious is carried as analogy in popular culture. This area is primarily concerned with the articulation of religious and theological metaphor to celebrity discourse. The interpretation of the theological in popular culture has been a growing area of research in recent years. Most of these studies, however, tend to focus on an aspect of the media as a potential dialogue partner for Christian thinking. This approach accepts that there are theological insights from the media and from popular culture but that these are accommodated within a Christian theological system. There are, however, some theologians who are examining the possibility of "theology" that is carried in popular culture in a way that is somehow disconnected from formal religious tradition. A good example of such a theologian is John Caputo.

Caputo argues for the possibility of what he calls "religion without religion." Formal religion has something that it is unable to restrict. "The traditional faiths," he says, "contain something that they cannot contain."[113] Religious phenomena are being seized and relocated in places where they are free from religions. One of the places this capture of the religious by nonreligion occurs is in the movies. Caputo gives as an example the *Star Wars* series. *Star Wars*, he says, "offers many young people today a high tech religious mythology, a fairly explicit 'repetition' or appropriation of elemental religious structures outside the confines of the institutional religious faiths."[114] Religious transcendence, he argues, has transcended the churches. God is not dead, he is alive and well in popular culture. As Heraclitus would say, "The gods are everywhere."[115]

At the root of Caputo's idea of religion without religion is the assertion that human experience has a "fundamentally religious quality."[116] Central to this is the idea that religious truth should be disassociated from the doctrine that a religion is the one true faith. According to Caputo, true religion is something different—it is related to being truly religious: "Religious truth is true with a truth that is of a different sort than scientific truth. Religious truth is tied up with being truly religious, truly loving God, loving God in spirit and in truth (John 4:24), and there are more ways to do that than are dreamt of by the faithful in the traditional confessions."[117] Religious truth, says Caputo, is a different kind of knowing—it is a "truth without knowledge." This is a knowing that does not enjoy a "privileged cognitive, epistemic, propositional information that has been withheld from others."[118] Religion without religion is the assertion of the medieval idea of religion as virtue. True religion means the virtue of being genuinely or truly religious.[119]

The idea of religion outside of religion is very suggestive, but it does seem rather a stretch to try and dignify celebrity culture as a kind of virtue or true religion. The theologian Tom Beaudoin is perhaps closer to the idea of a para-religion with the suggestion that religion in popular culture is characterized by what he calls an "irreverent spirituality." Beaudoin analyzes popular culture through its texts and practices to uncover a "lived" or "practical theology." This is a theology which he says is "both actual and potential"—actual in that it is being lived but potential in that it is also yet to be explored. He argues that irreverent spirituality or virtual faith is focused around four key themes: a suspicion of religious institutions, the sacredness of experience, suffering as a key to spirituality, and the ambiguity of spiritual life.[120] These themes "are not confined to the religious universe of the generation; they are the generation's gift and challenge to others, including religious institutions."[121] Through his analysis of popular culture Beaudoin is able to describe how religious traditions are altered through representation. As he puts it, "Gen X popular culture both reclaims forgotten themes and cloaks familiar ones in new images, de-familiarising them making them more acutely 'religious' again."[122]

Beaudoin illustrates the idea of irreverent spirituality through an analysis of Madonna's music video made to accompany her hit single "Like a Virgin" in 1984. In the video Madonna is shown dancing on a gondola, which is floating down a beautiful canal. She is wearing a long rosary as a necklace. The rosary, made of large beads, has a crucifix attached to it. As she dances on the boat, the rosary with its crucifix whips around her body. Beaudoin argues that Madonna, through this video, was one of the first contemporary pop artists to adopt the crucifix as a fashion statement.[123] In Generation X spirituality, he says, the crucifix appears regularly, but as with Madonna, the imagery and symbolism are never adopted in ways that neatly conform to Catholic tradition and theology. Rather, the use of this religious symbol is dislocated from its context and reframed through its association with the unfamiliar and the profane. Thus the rosary, which is more usually seen running through the hands of a pious nun or elderly spinster, is worn as decoration and display by a suggestively gyrating Madonna, who is telling us that she is "like a virgin touched for the very first time." The irreverent and indeed salacious use of religious iconography demonstrates the first of Beaudoin's key theological themes: that there is a deep suspicion of religious institutions in Gen X culture. He argues that this suspicion is evident in the video, played out through the provocative appropriation of the religious symbols of the rosary and crucifix.

Beaudoin illustrates the theological theme of "the sacredness of experience" with another video of Madonna's, "Like a Prayer." In the video Madonna is portrayed in what is clearly a Catholic church gazing through an iron gate at the statue of a black saint. He argues that the statue is probably a representation of the Dominican monk Martín de Porres, who lived in Peru at the end of the sixteenth and beginning of the seventeenth centuries and is celebrated for his concern for the poor. In Catholic devotion, de Porres has been associated with issues of racial justice.[124] Madonna is shown opening the gate and kissing the feet of the statue. Her touch brings the figure to life, and the newly animated black saint embraces Madonna and kisses her on the forehead.[125] Beaudoin argues that the video demonstrates the way that Gen X spirituality plays with Catholic imagery. The video is an example of the connections in popular culture between sensuality and Catholic symbolism. The emphasis on sensuality and the sexual is evidence of the way that Gen X spirituality prioritizes experience. Beaudoin argues, "As a key to religious living, Gen X reveres personal and communal experience by way of ripely irreverent expressions in popular culture. 'Like a Prayer' is at once a narrative of irreverence, a re-appropriation of Madonna's Catholic tradition, and a religious and social critique."[126]

At the close of the video the sensual intimacy between saint and pop star leads to a climax. The saint has once again become a statue, and it is possible that his animation has been a fantasy, but then Madonna discovers that blood is seeping from her hands and feet. She has received the stigmata. The significance is clear, says Beaudoin: Madonna, the liberator, is joined through sexual intimacy in a spiritual ecstasy with Saint Martín, and thereby she is connected to his fight for racial justice. This identification is ensured or guaranteed by the shedding of blood. There is a mystical identification in suffering and struggle. Beaudoin makes the link between this image of suffering and Christ as the suffering servant. To suffer, for Gen X, says Beaudoin, is to heighten experience, and it is the root to authenticity.[127]

Caputo and Beaudoin suggest that the religious persists in popular culture and that this can be traced in representation through a kind of theological analysis. Beaudoin's work relies on the complex nature of representation in popular culture. He draws attention to the way that songwriters, film directors, and music video producers routinely draw upon the theological. In his book *Virtual Faith*, Beaudoin draws attention to the way that popular culture is continually playing with the spiritual and the theological. Caputo makes a very similar obervation in his discussion of *Star Wars*. These theological treatments of popular culture seem to indicate not only that media discourses, far from being "secular," are often deeply religious but that the nature of this religion can be described through the analysis of the theological themes in representation.

PARA-RELIGION

We have used a variety of terms so far to suggest that celebrity culture, while it may have religious characteristics, is not in any formal sense a "religion." Celebrity culture has been spoken of as a form of degraded religion, or as a displaced religion. These approaches to religion in popular culture suggest how existing definitions of religion have to be stretched or made "fuzzy" to accommodate how the religious is changed in and through popular culture. It is very hard to see celebrity worship as a formal religion. In fact, the treatment of celebrity culture as a religious tradition, or indeed as a replacement for religious tradition, does not simply do a disservice to religion—it may well also run the risk not only of misrepresenting the lived experience of celebrity worship but of failing to see the religious significance of celebrity.

Para-religion is based on the premise that celebrity worship is not a religion but has religious parallels. Like the concept of para-social interaction, para-religion has the suggestion that religious elements are present but that they are experienced as a kind of contradiction. These religious elements are ambiguous and open to interpretation. The musicologist Marcel Cobussen adopts the term "para-spirituality" to describe the relationship between music and contemporary forms of spirituality. Para-spirituality, he says, is "an outside always already on the inside, an inflection of the spiritual as we usually regard it."[128] "Para," he suggests, is a "dangerous" prefix—it defies the rules of identity, stability, and centricity. It signifies "difference in sameness or sameness in difference," signifying at once proximity and distance, similarity and disparity, interiority and exteriority."[129] Para-spirituality, he suggests, "may refer to the absence of any predominating value of the spiritual or of ultimacy. The para-spiritual draws attention to a lack, to the space between, it indicates an incompleteness."[130] The para-spiritual is about "groping, hesitating, searching, not knowing, about abutting onto, brushing against, and intervening within, about the insight that the spiritual is unable to contain itself within itself and therefore needs the para-spiritual."[131] This means that attention must be paid not only to God but also to the devil, not only to Peter but also to Judas, not only to Mary the Mother of Jesus but also to Mary Magdelene, and not only to the Immaculate Conception but also to promiscuity.[132]

Para-religion is an attempt to account for similar kinds of ambiguities that appear in celebrity culture. In celebrity worship there are moments when the sacred appears to be present, but this is often subverted or interrupted by the irreverent. In celebrity culture the sacred appears to be present, but it has somehow been (sub)merged in the profane. In popular culture the processes of representation seem to appropriate theological analogies yet are twisted and altered in the process. Articulation lifts these theological metaphors and forms of expression from their relationship to any kind of formal religious community or tradition and relocates them in a conflicted, contested, contradictory, and fluid arena of meaning making. At the same time, references to the sacred are disconnected from any correspondence to divine transcendence and reconnected to a spirituality of the sacred self. This seems to describe a new form of religious context, but unfortunately these forms of representation and the kinds of identification that they support and elicit are all mixed up with a heavy dose of irony and, to use Beaudoin's term, irreverence. So any attempt to dignify celebrity worship as religion must somehow accommodate the pervading impression that anything to do with celebrity culture is somehow ephemeral and rather silly. Para-religion is an attempt to reconcile these various elements by developing a theory of a "sort of" religion.

PERSISTENCE OF THE THEOLOGICAL

Para-religion takes up Eliade's suggestion that the mythic persists in a degenerated or camouflaged form in popular culture.[133] Celebrity culture forms part of this residual mythic element in popular culture. So, just as it is possible to detect religious or theological elements in film, popular music, the Internet, and advertising, it is also possible to identify these religious elements in celebrity culture. Eliade's reference to camouflage and degenerate myths signals the way that the religious and the theological in celebrity culture are dislocated from any formal religious setting. There is no church of celebrity. Celebrity culture does not operate as a means to cement society, or as a part of an ongoing chain of meaning. All of these might indicate that celebrity culture is not a "religion." But this observation in itself does not mean that celebrity culture should be outside the parameters of concern for theology and religious studies. Para-religion identifies that, apart from formal religious traditions, there is a persistence of the mythic or the theological in popular culture and that celebrity culture is a key element in this.

The idea that there might be religion without religion is also helpful in understanding the religious in celebrity culture, but in para-religion the religion that is without religion is emptied of any concept of true faith. In celebrity culture what we see is the theological or the mythic without religion. Para-religion unhooks this connection to transcendence. The religious elements in celebrity culture draw upon the themes and metaphors from Christian theology, but these have been reformulated and reapplied. The ultimate concern of celebrity culture is a sacred self. For Durkheim, religion was society worshipping itself. Para-religion draws on this notion but disconnects from any relationship to a collective or any kind of church. The sacred self in celebrity culture does not generate the kind of cohesion suggested by Durkheim or Geertz as the basis of religion. In this sense celebrity culture is not a formal religion. At the same time, the persistence of the religious remains in the representation of celebrities and in the various practices and behaviors that shape consumption. Religion has been dislocated from tradition, the social, and the communal, but it remains the worship of the self, or more correctly, it is worship of the multiple possibilities of the self.

This reading of celebrity culture as worship of the self made sacred in representation draws on the idea of a subjective turn in contemporary religion. The shift toward the self that Woodhead and Heelas describe is writ large in celebrity culture. Celebrities present possibilities for the self; they represent the aspirational and the ideal as well as the fallen and the virtueless. Celebrities are meaningful because they offer ways of being human. These "ways" include the positive and the negative. Celebrities show perfection and they also show what it is to mess up as a human. As such they offer "subject positions" that may or may not be internalized by individuals. Through the processes of identification and disidentification celebrities function symbolically as sources of meaning and meaninglessness. The traces of transcendence that persist in popular culture correspond to the human, the sacred self. Celebrities are meaningful not because they represent a route toward the divine. They are icons, but not in the traditional sense, as windows onto eternity. Celebrities are icons that are more like mirrors. We simply see that we are the fairest, or at least we see the possible way that we might become the fairest in all the world. The "numinous" comes therefore not from "beyond" but from a collective within.

METAPHOR AND ANALOGY

For Hervieu-Léger and others, the notion of analogy and metaphor relates to the function of religion.[134] A sporting event can be seen as religious because it works in a similar way. Baseball, according to Chidester, is like religion because it does all the things that church does. Para-religion disconnects the idea of analogy from functionality. It does not argue that the sacred in celebrity culture functions as "religion." Rather it treats the idea of metaphor and analogy as the persistence of the theological. Celebrities attract to themselves certain terms and conventions of reference that are drawn mainly though not exclusively from Christian theology.

Theological references run through all areas of celebrity culture. Aspects of divinity become attached to the representation of celebrities. So celebrities come to symbolize an idealized view of the possibilities of human life, but in representation spiritual and theological analogies are articulated with their images and narratives. In this way celebrities become representative gods who reflect to us in an idealized form images of what it is to be human. Celebrities inhabit a material world that is simultaneously "enchanted" and heavenly. Although they live in this world as gods, goddesses, and demigods, their stories seem to tell an ever-recurring tale of apotheosis and magnificence that then turns to failure and collapse. These stories make continual use of analogy. Celebrities live the good life, they marry each other and have heavenly families, but they sin and they are unfaithful, they exhibit the results of moral and personal collapse, and very often they rise to new life in a process of redemption. In this sense the dying and rising god myth persists in celebrity culture, but it is void of its reference to the rejuvenation of life and the survival of society. It is a myth without effects, and we have gods without responsibilities.

In traditional theology we are subject to a God who sees all that we do and who will ultimately call us all to account. Through the media, however, our relationship with the divine has been reversed. We are now the ones who have the all-seeing powers. The gods cannot escape our agents with their photo lenses. We have our confessors who ask the intimate questions on the chat shows and in the magazines. Revelation is not the choice of the god—it is the demand of the people. We are the judges. We are the ones who weigh the actions of our gods. In the religion of the sacred self the self is divine arbiter. These kinds of judgments are fundamental to celebrity culture. We are continually invited to make decisions. Choices abound, whether it be between the way two stars are able to dance, or about which celebrity looks better on the catwalk. Minor arbitrations involve choices about what it is to be human. In other words, these choices form a debate about the self, the self that through analogy is "sacred." Choices in para-religion drift from the inane and the profane into the analogical and the theological. Celebrity culture exhibits a casual and a continual theological dispute that is rooted in the carnal and the material.

Occasional Epiphanies

Para-religion builds on Hervieu-Léger's distinction between the possibility of the sacred in popular culture and religion as a continuing tradition. It recognizes that celebrity culture does not constitute a religion, but it draws attention to the "traces" of the transcendent that persist in the popular. Gordon Lynch argues that the sacred persists in popular culture but that it becomes merged with the profane. The sacred is evident in particular thoughts, actions, and behaviors that constitute the relationship between people and the "object as sacred."[135] Para-religion develops this idea in two ways. First, it suggests a persistence of the religious in representation. The analogical and the metaphorical in celebrity discourse mean that there is a constant flow of the theological in the media. Secondly, para-religion sees as occasional the relationship between this flow of the theological and the worshipper. So while it is possible to see religious behavior and regard manifested in celebrity culture, there is no continuity or chaining that takes place which makes this religion or indeed that can be used as the basis for the constitution of celebrities as sacred.

The regard for the sacred does, however, appear often in unexpected ways. The mourning over Diana, for instance, took not only academics but everyone by surprise, including those who were involved in it. At sporting events or at rock concerts or other media-related events, a collectivity may be generated. This effervescence is evident and palpable, but it carries a certain enigmatic quality, an epiphany, a revealing of a communal regard or a greater than the sum of all that is present. This revealing, however, does not necessarily indicate a transcendent other, other than our sacred selves.

(Distracted) Meaning Making

Celebrity culture is fundamentally different from religion because no one takes celebrity culture seriously. Religions generally present themselves as being important. Religious people on the whole are "serious" about faith, and religious institutions are deadly serious. There is a "gravity" to religion that gives it weight. Religions are meaningful because they are "intent" on making a contribution. The idea of para-religion builds on Beaudoin's suggestion that religion in popular culture is fundamentally irreverent. Celebrity culture doesn't even pretend to be serious, and yet it operates as a source for meaning making and for identification. Religious devotion is based on the attention that is given by followers to religious traditions or figures. Celebrity culture, however, is characterized by a kind of inattention: it is flow of representation that we keep only half an eye on. We don't see celebrity culture as important or even meaningful, yet the stories seem to be part of our consciousness about the world. So the theological in celebrity representation is a theology that we largely ignore. Para-religion, therefore, does not appeal to the personal significance of celebrity as a form of the sacred or a meaningful sense of self—even though in some ways this may well be the case. What para-religion does is focus attention on our inattention and on how we are distracted and less than serious in our meaning making.

Here parareligion has some parallels with Geertz' idea that religion constitutes a system of meaning making. Celebrity culture does operate as a system of meaningful exchange within the discourses of popular culture. It is a key element in the symbolic language of the media. As a language it is "meaningful." At the same time, it is hard to dignify celebrity culture with the kind of weight that Geertz and others expect of religion.[136] Para-religion therefore needs to adopt something of Mazur's idea that the meaningfulness of popular culture is "fuzzy."[137] There is meaning making in celebrity culture, but it is meaning making that is nowhere near as serious as religious people would like or those who study religion would expect.

4

WHAT KIND OF GODS?

Celebrity culture is generated as a flow of images and stories in media representation. This representation is theological in nature, but it does not speak in a traditional way either about religion or about God. Christian thinking situates knowledge of God, or theology, in a narrative of relationship. John Calvin, for instance, begins his *Institutes of the Christian Religion* by saying, "Nearly all the wisdom we possess, that is to say, true and sound wisdom, consists of two parts: the knowledge of God and of ourselves."[1] For Calvin the key to "theology" lies in knowledge of the self in relationship to God. This relational element not only structures the knowing of God but also a right knowing of the self. Celebrity culture collapses these traditional theological distinctions into each other. Knowing self equals knowing God, who is a reflection of the self.

In celebrity culture the distinction between the self and the divine is blurred. One of the ways that this is manifested in discourse is through the adoption of theological metaphors and language as part of the structure of celebrity narratives. Thus celebrities become icons; stars are seen as "divine"; celebrities are "saviors"; celebrities sin, but they are also subject to judgment (by the tabloids); they are "sexy saints"; they find redemption and resurrect their careers. These theological themes are borrowed from traditional religious sources, but they are disconnected from any transcendent reference point. So the structure of a largely Christian theology remains, but it has been relocated in the theology of the self as divine. But as theological metaphors and analogies are articulated with celebrities, the meaning that they carry starts to shift and alter. So para-religion does not simply describe a dislocation or a degeneration of the religious in popular culture—it also connects to the way that theological metaphors are relocated and regenerated in popular discourse. It is not simply that celebrities are spoken of in analogous religious terms but that these theological metaphors are subtly altered in the process.

Ironic Attachments

In December 2009 when Tiger Woods made his confession of infidelity to the world, blogger Reasonable Robinson was quick to comment: "The announcement today that Tiger Woods is going to take an indefinite leave from golf appears to confirm his status as a Fallen Angel. He has lost his heavenly status in Brand Heaven."[2] This kind of religious analogy is very common in celebrity discourse. Another example from the blogosphere was found on Defamer, Gawker.com's Hollywood column, which greeted the new "*Forbes* 100 List of the World's Most Powerful Celebrities" with the headline "These Are Your Gods Now."[3] The *Forbes* list ranks celebrities according to their earnings during the year and their media visibility.[4] The Defamer blogger is condemnatory, convinced that the list is proof that we are worshipping false gods. *Forbes*' Top 100 is "Judgment-Summoning False Idolatry."[5] As part of the rehabilitation and publicity fightback of brand "Brangelina," the friends of actress Angelina Jolie also resort to religious analogy when they try to talk her up to the press. "Sources" are reported to have told the *National Enquirer* that "those who know her call her Saint Angie because of all the wonderful work she has been doing in Haiti," and "all her hard work in New Orleans seems to be finally paying off. She is being dubbed the 'Maid of Orleans.'"[6]

No one really believes that celebrities are saints, or that they are divine, or that they inhabit some kind of heavenly planet. The theological in representation operates as an analogy. The analogy, however, is not straightforward. Celebrity discourse uses religious metaphor with a heavy dose of irony. Tiger Woods is called a fallen angel with a knowing sense that he was never really an angel at all. His heavenly brand was always artifice. Some people may have been taken in for a time but with a false regard for a fake icon. Angelina Jolie may be represented as a saint or the Maid of Orleans, but this imagery carries within it the potential that everything will eventually go up in smoke. The gods of celebrity worship are false gods. They are idols.

The theme of idolatry is endemic in celebrity culture. It is not entirely insignificant that one of the longest-running top-rated celebrity shows in the U.S. and around the world is called *American Idol*. Despite its name this particular TV format is actually an invention of the British, where it was first screened as *Pop Idol* in 2001. Here again the knowingness of the theological reference can easily pass us by due to overfamiliarity. Theological reference has become routinized as part of the hegemony in celebrity culture. Alison Hill, like many others, is disgusted with the whole edifice. She quotes the Ten Commandments' prohibition on the worship of idols (Exod 20:1-6): "These 'graven images' God talks about could refer to modern day glossy magazines, the internet and the television, that bombard us daily with images of painted, pruned, coiffed, so-called beautiful 'stars,' and constantly inform us on what's cool, who's in, who's out, who's in rehab, who's adopting third world babies."[7] In contrast, *American Idol* invites us to worship. This is a worship that unashamedly declares itself as false. Here "idol" has double inflection—it is articulated with the way that the reality show reveals the process of "making" a pop star. We are invited to worship the manufactured pop star and to take pleasure in the way that our idol is made. At the same time, the word "idol" makes it clear that our worship is false and misplaced, and yet we are nevertheless invited to come and to adore. But we should not get too attached, because there will be another "idol" along very shortly.

(GRAVEN) IMAGES

In celebrity culture, image is power. Marilyn Monroe, for example, continues to exercise an influence on our imagination with her image, through which she appears to be always with us. She can be seen on T-shirts, calendars, mugs, wallpaper, and prints, in paintings, and in any number of photographs. Her movies are continually playing on a digital channel somewhere. Retouched and restored, her image continues to move and has life on DVD and Blu-ray. The reproduction of Marilyn ensures that her image remains in our consciousness. The marketing of Marilyn illustrates processes of mediation. These processes generate the divine—they take mere mortals and make them into deathless gods. It is the image that makes the individual into an idol. Through the technologies of representation our idols gaze upon us and we gaze upon them.

The reproduction of her image has transformed Marilyn into a modern-day "icon." John De Vito and Frank Tropea argue that through her image Marilyn has become an immortal icon.[8] The "immortal Marilyn"'s image generates a rich range of possible meanings. She is a vision of sexuality, frailty, femininity, and of course tragedy. Marilyn has a unique status as an icon because her image has been capable of attracting multiple layers of meaning, and through this complexity she has been an inspiration to a wide range of artists and creative people. De Vito and Tropea suggest that "Marilyn has played her greatest, perhaps most immortal, role of all, that of the divine muse, to artists like Andy Warhol, Willem De Kooning, and Claes Oldenburg. . . . [T]he depiction of Marilyn onstage, on-screen, on television, and in opera clearly reveals that her ultimate standing as an enduring cultural icon has not simply continued; it has over time increased and intensified to über-mythical proportions."[9]

Transformed into image, Marilyn can attract a variety of meanings. The mythic potential of celebrities such as Marilyn or Elvis or James Dean presents possibilities to artists and writers and filmmakers, but these possibilities are only there because the celebrity's image has the potential to fund multiple identifications. Cultural icons are made, but this making is more mysterious than the knowing irony of the reality TV show. Icons are not so self-evidently "idols." Their worship is slightly more reverent. Their making is shrouded in the kind of mystery that comes from "regard." Icons are imprinted on our consciousness— they are a constant reference point, a hook that we can hang things on. Commenting at the time of Michael Jackson's death, Gary Laderman said, "Americans look to the stars for guidance and inspiration, intimacy and ecstasy—powerful motives that bear on the sacred and can transform entertainment into revelation, escapism into liberation, and mortals into gods."[10] It is this regard that transforms celebrities into a "kind of" divine.

SELF-IMAGE

Celebrities are constantly occupied in self-promotion and grooming, says the blogger Alan Smithee. Some may believe in God, he says, but it is really themselves that attract their "worshipful affection." "I suspect that self-worship kind of comes with the territory in being a celebrity," says Smithee. "More or less a job requirement."[11] It is probably a sweeping generalization, but celebrities are more often than not obsessed with their image. The celebrity, says Sam Vaknin, typically exhibits all of the characteristics of the narcissist. Like Narcissus, the beautiful youth of ancient myth, celebrities appear to be transfixed by their own images. In the myth, the young man spurned the love of the nymph Echo, and his disregard for those who sought his love continued until one of his disappointed lovers prayed that he would experience rejection by someone he loved. One day Narcissus, we are told, came to a clear pool. There, as he stooped to drink, he fell in love with his own reflection. Recounts Robert Graves, "At first he tried to embrace and kiss the beautiful boy who confronted him, but presently recognized himself, and lay gazing enraptured into the pool, hour after hour."[12] Drawing on the Narcissus story, the pathological condition of narcissism refers to the absorption of the individual personality in the reflected approval of others. The celebrity narcissist, says Vaknin, is totally absorbed in achieving renown. There are no boundaries that someone afflicted with this pathology will not cross. For the narcissist there is "no such thing as bad publicity— what matters is to be in the public eye."[13] Says Vaknin, "Because the narcissist equally enjoys all types of attention and likes as much to be feared as to be loved, for instance—he doesn't mind if what is published about him is wrong ('as long as they spell my name correctly'). The narcissist's only bad emotional stretches are during periods of lack of attention, publicity, or exposure."[14]

In celebrity culture, the obsession with image is symbiotic. Celebrity images gaze at us from the media, and we in turn gaze at the celebrities who are intent on gazing at themselves. This is the mystical communion of the sacred self—a mutual indwelling of the self. We are taken up in regard for images that reflect ourselves. The figures portrayed in these images are themselves taken up with their own self-regard. The articulation of theological metaphors for this celebration of the self serves to sprinkle a mystical fairy dust on popular culture as the divine is emptied of its transcendent reference points and relocated in this self-regard. The appropriation of the divine by the human characterizes contemporary culture, but it has a very long history.

IMMORTALITY AND THE SACRED SELF

The idea of the self as divine or semidivine has its roots in the ancient world, and it has exercised power over the imagination ever since. In 1651 Thomas Hobbes wrote in *Leviathan* about the power of the ancient myths for those who seek glory:

> When a man compoundeth the image of his own person, with the image of the actions of an other man; as when a man imagines himselfe a *Hercules*, or an *Alexander*, (which happeneth often to them that are much taken with reading of Romants) it is a compound imagination, and properly but a Fiction of the mind . . . The *vain-glory* which consisteth in the feigning or supposing of abilities in ourselves, which we know are not is most incident to young men, and nourished by the Histories, or Fictions of Gallant Persons; and is corrected often times by Age and Employment.[15]

The first historical person to embody the ideals of the semidivine hero, according to the historian Leo Braudy, was Alexander the Great. Alexander, Braudy says, deserves to be called the first famous person. The pattern for Alexander's fame was found in the Homeric tradition. It is the *The Iliad* and *The Odyssey* that "embody the importance to the Greeks of the pursuit of an honour that will allow a man to live beyond death, as Hector says in the *Iliad* 'immortal, ageless all my days, and reverenced like Athens and Apollo.'"[16] It was this Homeric tradition that shaped and influenced the archetype for fame in the ancient world, and it was this legacy that inspired Alexander: "Like Achilles, he wanted fame through battle and conquest. But like Odysseus, he was constantly on the move, impelled by an urge to see and do more than any Macedonian or Greek ever had before."[17] It was not simply Alexander's achievements and conquests that contributed to his legend—it was his own identification with divinity. When he was the furthest east in his conquests, says Braudy, Alexander raised an altar to the twelve members of the Olympian family, a clear identification with Zeus, the head of the family of the gods. Before this, as Alexander conquered and then passed beyond the city of Nysa, he is said to have regarded himself as having surpassed Dionysius, who was by tradition the city's founder. These two figures, says Braudy, Zeus and Dionysus, represent the double divine inheritance that Alexander sought.[18] "In the later iconography," Braudy suggests, "his sculptured image—a flowing mane of hair, head twisted toward the left, eyes turned toward the sky—Alexander resembles an enraptured Dionysiac or an inspired poet."[19] Yet in his ability to conquer and rule the world Alexander has more of a resemblance to Zeus. Alexander actively encouraged those who were inclined to worship him by "fashioning" himself after the gods and demigods of ancient Greece. As the all-powerful ruler, he is part of a long tradition of pharaohs, caesars, and monarchs who have been seen as divine. By fashioning his image and its replication, Alexander pursued fame as an endorsement of his place among the heroes and the immortals.

Hollywood does not just make films about the ancient world—it has also appropriated the ancient world's mythic conventions. In celebrity culture, however, the ancient notions of the divine self are disconnected from the heroic and reconnected to fame. So in celebrity worship, ideas of the divine that are hard won in the ancient world are attributed to those who are just well-known. This is what Francesco Alberoni sees as the process by which stars are made through the "unconditional admiration and interest" of the crowd. The cry of the crowd—"You are a god!"—is an example of how the champion is seen as superior to all of those around him. Alberoni compares the adulation of the star to Max Weber's theory of charisma. For Weber, charisma is a "quality regarded as extraordinary and attributed to a person. . . . The latter is believed to be endowed with powers and properties which are supernatural and superhuman, or at least exceptional even where accessible to others, or again as sent by God, or as if adorned with exemplary value and thus worthy to be a leader."[20] The contemporary star is not strictly a "god." Stars do not wield power in the way that Weber describes. This does not preclude the famous racing cyclist becoming a "demigod" in the eyes of his enthusiastic fans, but it does not translate directly into other fields.[21] So as the divine self has been disconnected from the heroic it is also gently relieved of all responsibility.

ORDINARY GODS

In celebrity culture the divine self is articulated with fame. Heroic achievements, familiar from the Homeric myths and from stories of figures such as Alexander the Great, are no longer required. With them go all the notions of responsibility that are associated with charisma. In their place, divinity is connected to the representative nature of the star. The significance of the star, says Alberoni, lies in the way that his or her charisma operates as a symbolic reference point for society. Communities see themselves represented in individuals.[22] Through the development of the media, the focus for this representative significance of the star is shifted toward the personal and the private: "With the progress of visual information persons of the entertainment world begin, to an increasing degree, to make their mark. Their lives, their social relationships, become an object of identification or a projection of the needs of the mass of the population, a benchmark for positive or negative evaluation."[23] The power of the star, the star's divinity, lies in the way that he or she signifies or represents the ordinary and the personal. So the ancient notion of the transformation of the self through immortal acts has become the apotheosis of the star as ordinary because stars represent the aspirations of their audience. The divine self of the celebrity is therefore a reflection of those who worship the celebrity. The divine self in celebrity culture is the self of the audience transfigured and reproduced.

The shift toward the ordinary and personal as the focus for worship has taken a while to emerge. Richard Dyer argues that the star system in Hollywood was transformed by what he terms the "embourgeoisement of the cinematic imagination." This transformation started with the representation of stars as semidivine, screen gods and goddesses. Gradually these "heroes" were seen as "identification figures, the embodiment of typical ways of behaving."[24] This meant that the stars became less directly the representation in film of particular virtues and vices. The archetypes of the cinema—the vamp, the clown, the good girl, the landlord, the villain—gave way to more individuated characterization.[25] The introduction of psychological realism in film led to the interest in the "real lives" of the stars and hence to the explosion in magazines and media coverage of what was previously seen as personal and private. This "intimate vision with its attendant obsession with persons" is one of the "most pervasive conditions characterising social life under modern capitalism."[26] The interest in the personal and the private does not, however, erode the divine status of the star. It simply relocates this status into the ordinary and the social. The star does not cease to be seen as semidivine, but the exceptional and the special are combined with the ordinary and the ideal is located in the everyday.[27]

The shift toward the ordinary in Hollywood leads to the concentration on the personal. In celebrity culture the ordinary and personal becomes itself distanced from the need for any specific achievement or skill. The focus on the personal and the private becomes the substance of representation. The divine self, reflected in the narratives and images of the celebrities, becomes a self of the ordinary rather than a self of the heroic. The celebrity has a responsibility, but this is a responsibility simply to maintain himself or herself as "image." We watch them to see how well they do with their weight loss and weight gain, how they manage their relationships, and how they make choices in the minefield that is fashion. Stars are ordinary, but it is their ordinariness that acts as the lightning rod for our attention. Morin says, "The stars are like the gods: everything and nothing. The divine substance that fills and crowds this nothingness is human love. The god's infinite void is also an infinite richness not his own. The star is empty of all divinity, as are the gods. The star is full of all humanity, as are the gods."[28]

THE PANTHEON OF GODS

The self as the divine in popular culture gives birth to a multiplicity of possible gods. Here again are parallels with the ancient world. The media elevate people into the pantheon of the gods, and as in the Roman Empire their images are sent around the world, says the religious journalist

Andrew Brown. This "repeated apotheosis" makes our popular culture "more like paganism than it is comfortable to admit."[29] Celebrity culture is based around a series of stories about these figures. It is "more a set of interlocking and often contradictory stories," he says, "rather than a coherent theology."[30] The result is, according to Brown, that two figures such as Princess Diana and Jade Goody may be different archetypes, or they may indeed be the same deity, worshipped through different images. Both Diana and Jade have been acknowledged after their deaths as "aspects of the Celebrity of Compassion, a deity a bit like the Buddha of Compassion, but a whole lot easier to photograph."[31] Jade's transformation is traced back to her time in the *Big Brother* House, when in the *Sun* newspaper's 2002 coverage of her she was called "the most hated woman in Britain." Seven years later, covering her funeral, the *Sun* had changed its tune: "Not since the funeral of Princess Diana had a nation been so united in grief. Once again people felt they had lost one of their own."[32]

Celebrities do not carry fixed meanings. They are gods on whom we project the possibilities of what it is to be human. The result is that celebrity worship is a kind of polytheism in which we worship a pantheon of gods, demigods, and mortals. Like the immortals of the ancient world, these figures combine admirable characteristics with weakness and failings. So we see in our newspapers parallels with Zeus, who is all-powerful and yet inclined to a kind of sexual addiction. Zeus is locked into a dysfunctional marriage with his jealous and vengeful wife, Hera. This kind of narrative is repeated again and again in celebrity culture, with an ever-changing cast of actors. As the meanings attached to celebrities shift and change, we see characters appearing in the media who remind us further of the tales of Mount Olympus. There are actors, artists, and musicians who seem to embody something of Bacchus, with his aura of spirituality and his predilection for excess. There is the modern-day Hercules who is laboring over his latest challenge, and we know he is doing so to compensate for a former weakness. Finally, we are treated to a continual parade of women who fulfill or aspire to be some kind of Venus. These kinds of parallels support Mircea Eliade's suggestion that there is a persistence of the mythic in contemporary culture. He argues, as we have seen in the previous chapter, that the myths continue but in a "camouflaged form" in the "dream factory" of the cinema. In celluloid we see "the fight between hero and monster, initiatory combats and ordeals, paradigmatic figures and images (the maiden, the hero, the paradisal landscape, hell and so on)."[33] Morin also sees a direct parallel between the cinema and the myths of ancient Greece and Rome. Stars, he says, are "anthropomorphic gods"—they are constructed from both the stuff of life and that of dreams.[34] Says Morin, "The star is of the same double nature as the heroes of mythologies—mortals aspiring to immortality, candidates for divinity, tutelary spirits, half men and half gods."[35]

Celebrities are part of this process whereby the sacred is merging with popular culture. They make up a kind of re-enchantment of the world. Celebrities re-enchant the world because they are "myth bearers; carriers of the divine forces of good, evil, lust and redemption."[36] In a world that has been disenchanted through the rationalism and secularization of the Enlightenment, celebrities reoccupy the places that have been left by deities and power up the spaces where the power of the gods has appeared to wane. Deena Weinstein and Michael Weinstein are much more critical of this manifestation of the sacred in popular culture. They see celebrity worship as a false construct. It is weak religion, an inauthentic and misleading substitute for traditional belief: "It satisfies spiritual needs with a weak religion that allows us to worship the best, the worst, and the most banal of ourselves."[37] Celebrities form a cluster of different representations of the self as divine beings. The "cult" of celebrity, Weinstein and Weinstein argue, can be interpreted as a new form of polytheism. Through renown and achievement, people are taken up in the media and come to represent human virtues and characteristics: "There are celebrities for all of the major interests, fears, and desires of human life."[38] So as with polytheistic religions, in celebrity culture we have a range of divine figures that personify aspects of human nature. These personifications of the self are multiple, various, and often contradictory.[39] Celebrities make up a pantheon of ever-changing "sub-deities who cavort and contend with each other."[40] The "comings and goings and ruptures and couplings" of these figures form the equivalent of the mythic tales of the gods.[41]

Celebrity Saints

In medieval popular devotion, the saints were seen as kindly neighbors. They were, says the historian Eamon Duffy, "friends and helpers":[42]

"The saints that gazed out from the screens and tabernacles of late medieval England were often emphatically 'kind neighbours, and of our knowing,' country people themselves, like St James the Great at Westhall, with his sensible shoes, hat and staff, or St Anthony, on the same screen with his friendly pig."[43] Friendship with the saints reveals not only devotion but a close identification on the part of the worshipper. The saints were envisioned as ordinary, close to the life of the faithful. Prayerful and devoted relationships demonstrate, says Duffy, a "sort of affectionate dependence," and this was "clearly the result of particular devotion on the part of the client who 'adopted' specific saints in the hope that he or she would be adopted and protected in turn."[44]

Just as there are parallels between the myths of Greece and Rome and celebrity culture, there are similar connections to the cult of the saints. Braudy argues that celebrities are more akin to the Christian saints than to other kinds of spiritual authorities. So Tiger Woods could be seen as the patron saint of golfers; or Jimmy Carter might be the protector of down-home liberal farmers. "Celebrities have their aura—a debased version of charisma" that stems from their all-powerful captivating presence, Braudy says.[45] Celebrities offer a focus for a particular kind of inspiration and identification in ways similar to the medieval saints. Celebrities "motivate us to make it."[46] A celebrity like Oprah Winfrey is a role model. Oprah suffered through poverty, sexual abuse, and racial discrimination, but she eventually became the wealthiest woman in media. The cyclist Lance Armstrong survived advanced testicular cancer and went on to win the Tour de France seven times.[47] Speaking at the time of Michael Jackson's death, Gary Laderman suggested that the singer's life story, although it has many troubling aspects, may become a "morality play": "Like other saints, he will be forgiven by his public, and I expect he will become an inspiration and role model, in some ways, for those who want to make music, become famous, or leave a mark in this world."[48] So like the saints of a previous era, celebrities offer an encouragement and a friendly presence and support. Their lives may perform a similar inspiring function as those of the saints. Unlike the cult of the saints, however, there are no specific religious practices associated with this kind of identification. Sainthood, therefore, is a limited analogy. Celebrities can be likened to saints, but celebrity culture does not operate as a religious practice in the same way.

Contradictory Gods

Celebrity culture produces an ever-changing array of gods, saints, and demigods. The pantheon of celebrity figures is articulated with various theological themes, and their stories are structured around theological metaphors. These theological themes and metaphors, however, do not form a coherent system. Celebrities represent a wide variety of possible selves. The result is a vision of the divine self in a variety of guises, both positive and negative. Celebrities have offered us a distinctive view of the world. This is a version of reality where the possibilities appear to have no limits. We are shown a future where anything and everything is possible.[49] Celebrities are the "living proof of this"—they represent how ideas such as "restraint, prudence, and modesty have either been discredited or just forgotten. Celebrity culture has replaced them with impetuosity, frivolity, prodigality."[50] These characteristics were once regarded as morally problematic. But celebrities, says Cashmore, have replaced virtues with vices.[51]

The view of the divine that is seen in a celebrity "theology" is therefore very similar to the ancient myths. Celebrities, like the Greek and Roman gods, appear to manifest both the noble and the venial. The gods fall out with one another, they get jealous, and they exact revenge. These gods represent not simply the possible good or the ideal, they also appear to manifest the profane and the fallen. Celebrities represent opposite and opposing possibilities for the self. Theological metaphors do not operate as a form of order or as a transcendent reference point. The sacred self reflected in the representation of celebrities presents our own conflicted view of ourselves. The contradictory nature of the representation takes us into the conflicted and complex negotiations involved in constructing the self in contemporary culture. Identification with the celebrity is not the only way that this process takes place. Disidentification is at least or perhaps even more significant because in our disapproval we are drawn into an engaged and engaging reaction to celebrity culture. These negative responses not only reveal our values, they connect us to others who have similar views. The tabloid papers exploit these communities of

disidentification even more than they do those of identification. The contradictory nature of celebrity culture finds a unity only to the extent that
the various possibilities of the human that are represented by celebrities
allow for a changing point of reference in the construction of the self.

SEXY GODS

The divine in celebrity culture is highly sexualized. Here again there
are significant parallels with Greek and Roman mythology. Robert
Graves refers to "Amorous Zeus," who lay not only with numerous
nymphs but with mortal women as well. Zeus was to father four of
the Olympian deities, says Graves, out of wedlock.[52] As we have seen,
Zeus appears to have something in common with celebrities in contemporary culture in that he seems to have a sex addiction problem. Zeus,
like the contemporary sportsman or film star, represents a powerful
divinity that may rule over all he sees, who already has a beautiful
wife and a wonderful home but is not prevented by this from sneaking
off to cheat with someone else.

Celebrity culture merges the theological with the profane in a manner that is very similar to that seen in the ancient myths. The reflected
self that we see in celebrity culture combines the sexual with the theological. Paris Hilton seems to exemplify the way that sex plays such a
significant role in the celebrity version of the "theological." As discussed
in chapter 2, the heiress Paris Hilton has achieved a kind of hegemony in
media coverage over the last few years. Her rise to fame was ensured by
the notorious release of a sex tape featuring Paris in intimate moments
with her then boyfriend. The leaking of the sex tape and its subsequent
sale, despite the threats of legal action by her family, ensured that Paris
gained maximum publicity. Cynthia Cotts of the *Village Voice* wrote following the scandal, "Serious news outlets were scrutinizing a celebrity
who had done nothing to merit the attention. . . . Two talking points
emerged: Why do we care, and how exactly has the tape hurt this girl's
reputation?"[53] As Cashmore points out, the answer to these questions
lies in Cotts' own article. We care because the media are covering the
story, and the coverage in itself made Paris a celebrity star. Sex sells
newspapers and magazines, and provided it is not seen as "cheating" or
infidelity, sex does a celebrity no harm at all. Paris' exploitation of her

sexuality is one of the reasons why her "image" has become so significant. It is not simply the fact that she is "putting out" for the public. Paris
is seen as someone whom women and particularly young girls identify
with. She symbolizes not simply the sexualized nature of celebrity culture but more importantly how sex and sexual power and attraction are
key themes in the negotiation of the self. Paris, Marilyn Monroe, Lady
Gaga, Angelina Jolie, and all the myriad of sexy and sexualized women
in the celebrity pantheon are a pert(inent) reminder that sex is a fundamental theme in celebrity worship.

The link between religious representation in celebrity culture and
the sexual is perhaps seen most clearly in Princess Diana. Diana was no
saint, or at least she was not a saint in the traditional sense of the word.[54]
In terms of traditional Christian morality, her sex life meant that she
could be regarded as a sinner. Diana was a self-confessed adulteress
who abandoned her husband. Lord Coggan, the former archbishop of
Canterbury, called her a "false goddess with loose morals."[55] Diana was
a "goddess" because she represented something significant to people, but
Coggan made a link to the sexual. Diana had loose morals. So the "theological" metaphor is connected to the sexual.

Diana is a type for a new kind of sainthood: "Whether she is seen
as a feminist icon, a symbol of maternal love or single motherhood, a
nationalist heroine, a sign of hope for the dispossessed and the suffering
around the globe, a unifying point for minority groups and the mar-
ginalised, the lonely, the poor, the sick, Diana is always turned into a
saint, a post modern saint."[56] She is postmodern not simply because her
transformation is constructed through a range of different narratives
and images but because she relocates sainthood. Hers is a sainthood
that is not forged from asceticism and self-denial. Rather it is found in
desire. Diana is seen as both desired and desiring.[57] Diana is an archetype of desire. Her care for others comes from this core, and in turn
she is also desired as an unattainable other. Her position as saint comes
from the perception of her own suffering. Her care for others was recognized from her own costly personal suffering.[58] For the journalist Julie
Burchill, Diana is the icon of "sexy-saintliness." "Diana," she says, "is
the Church of England at play in high heels. She is Madonna crossed
with Mother Teresa—a glorious totem of western ideals."[59]

In Diana we can see an illustration of what Hoover calls the convergence of religion and media in popular culture. Hoover's point is that it appears that media and religion are starting to occupy the same spaces.[60] In notions such as sexy saintliness and the goddess with loose morals, this convergence can be seen to be taking place as the articulation of the theological with the profane, the divinization of the sexual. This connection is operative at the level of discourse. It is a re-embedding of the theological in the venial.

GODS WHO FAIL

Heroes and gods are not celebrated simply for their unique qualities or accomplishments—we also observe and enjoy them as they fail and as they fall from grace. The ancient myths tell of those who succumb to their own nature and those who are subject to fate. So for instance there is Oedipus, who is fated to murder his own father and to marry his mother; and Hercules, who becomes insane and then murders his own children.[61] Celebrity culture has its share of murder and sexual wrongdoing, but many of the failures are more mundane: drugs, booze, assaulting people in nightclubs, and the occasional wardrobe malfunction. These minor iniquities, however, show us that the gods who people the world are gods who fail.

The failure of the gods does not only apply to those who are the victims of events, it also includes those who succumb to their own imperfect nature. These failures, however, often seem to make celebrity figures more accessible to the public. We identify with gods who mess up. A good example of this is Princess Diana's widely reported struggle with eating disorders and low self-esteem. These weaknesses meant that Diana came to represent a range of possible identifications for women. For the feminist critic Diana Simmonds, Diana's iconic status is a disaster: "Diana Spencer, aristocrat, ordinary girl and scholastic failure has achieved the impossible status—not only of Fairy Princess and Virgin Mother, but also the magical Size Ten. She is the disastrous heroine of the eighties."[62] The revelation that Diana's ideal figure may have had its origins in her anxiety only served to cause more irritation to Simmonds. Diana had managed to transform ordinariness into the extraordinary. Her ability to behave like us even when she was dressed so glamorously and in the public gaze enhanced her stardom and celebrity status.[63] Diana's successes and her failures are seen as iconic because they appear to represent significant aspects of the experience of women. Diana "signifies something, whether positive or negative, about the changing status of women; and finally because her femininity and celebrity can be linked in some way to the state of the culture and signs of the times."[64]

IMPERFECT GODS

The gods of celebrity culture not only fail, they appear at times to not really amount to very much. It does not require a particular talent to be a celebrity. Some do have a skill, but this is not the reason why they attract our attention. As Cashmore asks, "are we fascinated by Tom Cruise because of his dramatic performances, or because of his weird affiliation with Scientology, his stern repudiation of the suggestion that he is gay, and his serial marriages?"[65] Reality TV stars have no obvious talents, but once they have made it into the celebrity market they can live by offering the same product "that makes Hollywood actors, and global rock stars celebrities; not talent but presence."[66] What keeps a celebrity a celebrity is the ability to appear with regularity on chat shows, in advertising, and in newspapers, magazines, and Internet sites. It is our interest in them that makes celebrities significant.

There is a Faustian pact that takes place between the media and the celebrity. The expectation is that the celebrity must reveal himself or herself in intimate and lurid detail. In return the celebrity receives fame, riches, and a fabulous lifestyle. The consumer in and through this deal is given the chance to feast on celebrities' inner souls.[67] This bargain offers a "temporary divinity," but it is not an attractive industry. Inside knowledge of the celebrity industry is not for the squeamish: "Like the making of sausage or violin strings, the minting of celebrity is not a pretty business."[68] This deal is laid bare with Princess Diana, who appeared to have everything: wealth, beauty, a husband who was a prince, and Elton John for a friend. Yet she revealed herself to be needy and vulnerable. She was cherished because the public regarded her neediness as being as "desperate and as formless as their own."[69] Celebrities like Diana are "anthropomorphic gods."[70] The star is human, and the processes of divinization remain "profane."[71] "The stars' divinity is ephemeral."[72] It is a mixture of the sacred and the profane. "The star is divinised in spite of her evident 'humanity,' in spite of her submission to the outrages of time, in spite of the aesthetic consciousness of the spectator, who knows that the star is playing a role in the cinema and not a living person."[73] The anthropomorphic gods of the celebrity pantheon reflect not simply the aspirations of their fans—they also represent the anxieties, insecurities, and downright bad luck that is part of daily life for many people. Celebrities are imperfect gods because they are ourselves writ large.

Powerless Gods

We are used to the way that the characters in ancient myth are taken up and used in a variety of ways. In art and literature ancient myths function as reference points, but their truth often lies in their use within the work of art or the text of the poem, novel, or play. Myths represent a theology that can be molded and shaped by the user. The significance of the ancient myths lies in the way that they have been taken up and used. Celebrity gods in a similar way are only significant because of the way that they are taken to mean something by audiences.

Celebrities, says Alberoni, are a "powerless elite." They are a class of entertainers "whose institutional power is very limited or non-existent, but whose doings and way of life arouse considerable and sometimes a maximum degree of interest."[74] Celebrities are famous, and they earn considerable sums of money; they are able to influence politicians and the wider public, but this ability to influence is based almost entirely on image. The image of the celebrity can be manipulated and used in a variety of ways to sell products and services. It may even be used to generate an interest in charitable causes or issues such as climate change or the destruction of the rain forest, but this is not the same as having the ability to make decisions and wield political power.

The symbolic or theological "power" that characterizes celebrity is not ontological. The significance of an individual celebrity does not arise from his or her "essence," rather it lies outside of that celebrity in the regard of others. Celebrities are not gods, they are made gods, and they can be unmade as gods. The gods in celebrity culture are part of a para-religion. There is no church of celebrity. The theological as it is formed and circulated in media representation does not stimulate any kind of steady "devotion." On one level the theological is just there, it is part of the backdrop to life as it is experienced in popular culture. At times the celebrity god may be taken up as significant, and at other points we regard him with a kind of cynical disregard. Here also are some parallels with the myths of the ancient world. Despite the fact that the gods of Greece and Rome have long been dislocated from their original contexts in the religious life and observance of the ancient world, they continue to be significant. The stories and the characters from the ancient world have been an enduring reference point for literature and art long after they ceased to function as a religious system. Celebrity narratives operate in a similar way. Writing in the early part of the nineteenth century, poet Samuel Taylor Coleridge speaks of the continuing significance of the ancient gods and demigods:

> The intelligible forms of ancient poets,
> The fair humanities of old religion,
> The Power, the Beauty, and the Majesty
> That had their haunts in dale or piny mountain,
> Or forest, by slow stream, or pebbly spring,
> Or chasms and watery depths; all these have vanished;
> They live no longer in the faith of reason;
> But still the heart doth need a language; still
> Doth the old instinct bring back the old names;
> Spirits or gods that used to share this earth
> With man as with their friend; and at this day
> 'Tis Jupiter who brings whate'er is great,
> And Venus who brings every thing that's fair.[75]

These are gods who represent something significant without commanding a cult. They can be a point of reference, an archetype, but they have ceased to be compelling deities. They are gods we can ignore if we choose.

Religion requires a level of belief in religious figures and a certain regard for a god. Celebrity culture is a kind of para-religion. It is characterized by attention but attention without respect—an irreverent attention. Consumers know, says Cashmore, that the celebrities they follow are rather "insubstantial" and "inconsequential."[76] "We know that so-and-so became famous because she slept (and told) with someone who was vaguely a 'Somebody,'" says Cashmore. "And that a former reality show's contestant earns several million a year in spite of a self-acknowledged absence of intellect, taste, knowledge, skill or anything worthy of merit."[77] Celebrities may shy away from revealing the vast sums that are spent for their own promotion on the fashion shoots; the glossy coverage of their homes and holidays; the huge effort that goes into music video production or fly-on-the-wall, behind-the-scenes coverage, but consumers know about this. We just choose to ignore it, says Cashmore. We know that the whole celebrity phenomenon is a media-fabricated bubble with little substance, and yet we still choose to follow the lives of these people. Knowing that it is fake is part of the attraction: "The pleasure in being in celebrity culture is that the consumer observes, secure in the knowledge that he or she is actually not just an observer, but a player too."[78]

Celebrity media reflect and encourage the irreverent disdain for the celebrity gods. The coverage of celebrities since the 1950s, says Joshua Gamson, has focused not simply on the star but on the processes that build the star-making system. We know about agents and producers and the various negotiations between journalists and those they interview. The entertainment industry has become part of what is revealed in the story. This knowingness means that the audience begins to be instructed in viewing not simply stars and their private lives but also the processes that present these "fabrications." Says Gamson, "Armed with knowledge about the process, the audience doesn't need to believe or disbelieve the hype, just to enjoy it."[79] Celebrity gods do not require "belief" or indeed any particular devotion. They live out their lives in the Mount Olympus of media land. They sport and play, and we check them out from time to time. In all of this we are aided and abetted by the celebrity media. Through *People* magazine, the *National Enquirer*, *Hello!*, and *Heat*, we are given a window into the Elysium of the gods. Our gaze, however, is privileged, laced with cheek and superiority. Su Holmes argues that *Heat* magazine is a text permanently "parked in expose gear."[80] The magazine describes itself as "brimming with tongue in cheek humour" and as demonstrating a "trademark irreverent style."[81] The magazine alternates between presenting celebrities as style icons for its female readers and presenting them with a kind of mockery. The magazine therefore gives style tips alongside such items as "The Best and the Worst," comparing the fashion horrors with stars seen to have got it right. The many celebrity photos also exhibit these two aspects of respect and irreverence. So for every picture of a celeb looking good there are several which concentrate on spots, weight problems, underarm sweat patches, and so on.[82] Holmes suggests that the magazine's use of irony and irreverence is a kind of negotiation: *Heat* demonstrates a knowing realization that all celebrity culture is fake and a fabrication, but in acknowledging and making this very clear the magazine also seems to obscure or hide the questions, which relate to why celebrities are "fetishized, debated and admired."[83]

"Sort of" Gods

The theological significance of celebrity gods does not lie in what they reveal about the divine. A theology of celebrity culture in this sense is not the same as, for instance, a traditional Christian theologian talking about the "theological" in relation to popular culture. We learn little if anything from celebrity theology about the Christian God or indeed the gods of any formal religion. What we do see is a reflection of ourselves—as divine. This is not society worshipping itself but the collective regard and disregard of individuals as they interact with representation in the media. The theological in celebrity culture represents our conflicted and complex self clothed in the metaphors of the divine and reflected back to us. The gods in celebrity culture offer us a take on the divine that is distinctive and quirky. This is a theology in which there is not one god but many gods. These gods, moreover, may represent contradictory and opposing values. Celebrity worship combines the sacred and the profane. We worship ourselves not simply as we wish ourselves to be but also as we see ourselves failing, being imperfect and unworthy of worship. The gods of celebrity culture play out their narratives with a certain intensity and profligacy, but we have only half an eye upon them. We take up our gods as and when it suits. We do not feel in any way compelled to worship. In fact we may be skeptical worshippers, cynical worshippers, and distracted worshippers. Celebrity worship reveals the extent to which we are conflicted about ourselves—however much we try to attach a religious balm to our wounds.

There is little point in seeking a coherent theological worldview or a systematic theology from celebrity worship. What we do see are snapshots of the gods, the demigods, and our sexy saints. These visions are generated through the use of religious and theological metaphor. The theological works solely as an analogy. These theological themes are significant because they offer a glimpse of the possible self, the self that we both identify with and disidentify with. These themes also show how what might be construed as a dislocated or camouflaged religion actually works. The religious, through articulation in media representation, is being altered. This process does not tell us anything that we can directly identify as "religion," rather it offers a glimpse of the way that the sacred persists and is actually mutating and reproducing in popular culture. The attraction of the theological as analogy does not simply tell us about the sacred self, it also reveals how the notion of the divine and a transcendent God is problematized through the articulation of irreverence and irony. The knowing sense that the regard for celebrities is a form of idolatry and the tongue-in-cheek appropriation of religious terms for our celebrity gods change the theological representation associated with traditional religion. To speak of sexy gods and cultural icons on one level delivers a veneer of significance. The other side of this, however, is that it hints at the way popular culture is conflicted about notions of transcendence.

There is a distinct possibility that theological and religious analogies in celebrity culture indicate that the sacred may be shifting in popular culture. Most significantly, the divine is now located in the human. This is an incarnational understanding that locates the divine not in one human being but in all humanity. This is a divinity that inhabits "flesh" in all the senses of the word. God and the sexual are merged, and desire and worship are mixed in a potent cocktail. Just as there is no distinction between the sacred and the profane in our sexualized vision of celebrities, there is also a willingness to embrace fallibility. The celebrity gods behave badly, they mess up, but they also triumph through suffering and transform their situations by rising above their circumstances. The appropriation of theological and religious metaphors in celebrity culture therefore offers an indication that the ideas of the sacred and of the divine are undergoing a significant change. This change is taking place outside of formal religious traditions. It is a theological creativity and construction that operates in popular culture. It is para-religion.

5

THEMES

Meryl Streep has turned sixty. She has dominated the headlines, says the journalist Shane Watson. She has refused plastic surgery, she is now starring in a film in which her character has sex, and "she eats carbs all the time, knocks back the booze, wears her hair messy, and generally defies all the rules of making it as a modern woman, never mind a Hollywood star."[1] Sharon Stone, who has clearly taken a very different approach to her self-image, is reported to have called Streep "an unmade bed." Watson observes that Stephanie Beacham, Ivana Trump, Dannii Minogue, Victoria Beckham, and Cheryl Cole are on the side of Sharon Stone on this one. This has nothing to do with age, says Watson, "It's about the Unmade Beds versus the Pristine Pillows—two different types of women with different styles."[2] The Unmade Beds also include Tilda Swinton, Helen Mirren, Stella McCartney, and Kristen Stewart. Unmade Beds like dogs, they eat cake, and while they may own a hairdryer, they rarely use it. Watson sees herself in this category, but the Pristine Pillows, she says, have been in the ascendancy: "We in the UB category have come under a lot of pressure over the past decade to conform to the prevailing PP standard; so, every so often, we'll have a manicure, or get a really serious bikini wax, or diet ourselves into some impossibly teeny jeans. We've even been known to get our teeth whitened." Watson recognizes that Unmade Beds may be disorganized, but she concludes by saying that when she has to choose between Stone and Streep she knows "which side of the bed she would rather be on."[3]

Almost twenty years before Watson's article, Meryl Streep features in an article that explores a very similar area to do with women and the politics of identification and disidentification. Camille Paglia is praising Elizabeth Taylor, whom she calls "Hollywood's Pagan Queen": "My devotion to Elizabeth Taylor began in the late Fifties, when I was in junior high school and when Taylor was in her heyday as a tabloid diva. I was suffering sustained oppression in the Age of Perky Blondes: day after day, I reeled from the assaults of Doris Day, Debbie Reynolds, Sandra Dee. All that parochial pleasantness! So chirpy, peppy, and pink, so well-scrubbed, making the world safe for democracy."[4] For Paglia, Elizabeth Taylor was the antidote. She was the "pre-feminist woman" who used the sexual power that feminism has tried to explain but never managed to destroy. Taylor connects us to feminine archetypes; in her we see Delilah, Salome, and Helen of Troy. In Taylor, Paglia says, "[a]n electric, erotic charge vibrates the space between her face and the lens. It is an extra-sensory phenomenon."[5] This "pagan eroticism" is compared by Paglia to what she calls the Protestantism of Streep. Meryl Streep is fixated on the words, says Paglia. She "flashes clever accents to mask her failures." If her work was dubbed for a movie audience in India there would be nothing left, says Paglia, "just that bony earnest horse face moving its lips."[6] Streep would be incapable of playing the great mythological roles. She could never be Cleopatra. Taylor, however, is a creation of the world of show business. She has the "hyperreality" of a dream vision. Streep's actorly manner is a boring decorum beside the earthy sensuality of Taylor. Says Paglia, "I'll take trashy, glitzy Old Hollywood any day. Elizabeth Taylor heartily eating, drinking, lusting, laughing, cursing, changing husbands, and buying diamonds by the barrel, is a personality on a grand scale . . . Elizabeth Taylor is woman in her many lunar phases, admired by all the world."[7]

JUDGMENT—WHO GOES YOU DECIDE

What is at stake in celebrity culture is not so much what we think of Meryl Streep or Sharon Stone or Elizabeth Taylor but what we think of ourselves. What is being debated is the kind of life we should live and how we should live it. It is the intersection of style and ethics, decorum and discipleship. We are asked to choose our gods and then we are invited, or indeed enticed, to sit in judgment upon them. Celebrity discourses routinely position the audience as divine arbiter. Here the symbiosis of the sacred self appears again. Celebrities are sacred because they represent the sum of the possibilities for the self. Through representation these possible selves are reflected back to us as image and idol, and we are asked to choose between them. Our judgments concerning different celebrities become an arena to negotiate identity—our possible or ideal self. So the discussions and debates that make up the tittle-tattle of celebrity coverage take us into our sensibilities about our own self. The articulation of religious and theological analogies to this conflicted and contested process of identification and disidentification on one level only serves to legitimate the profane by invoking the sacred. At the same time, however, as popular culture and the theological merge, religious language undergoes a subtle change. Judgment in celebrity culture is fundamental to this process because it draws us into an engagement. It invites us to take a view and to occupy a position.

This week, one of our national newspapers is asking us the engaging question "Julia Right to Bare Her Mum Tum?" Beside the headline is a picture of Julia Roberts; she is wearing a bikini that is rather reminiscent of the green polka-dot dress she wore in the movie *Pretty Woman*. She is running along the beach wearing a smile and a huge pair of sunglasses. The *Sun* lays it on the line: "Julia Roberts must be the bravest lady in Hollywood. She dared to bare her mummy midriff in a skimpy bikini in Hawaii this week. The 41-year-old Pretty Woman star gave birth to twins Hazel and Phinnaeus four years ago and Henry, just 22 months ago—and proved to the public she wouldn't go near a surgeon's knife to get a 'perfect' bod back. But is her look tum-thing special or does it turn your stomach?"[8] The newspaper then sets out the case for and against Julia'a mum tum. The journalist Nick Francis is clear. Roberts looks in very good shape for a woman of forty-one. She is happy and seems to be more healthy now that she has a slightly fuller figure. OK, argues Francis, her tummy might have more of a "bounce" than it once did, but that just makes "a screen legend more of real person."[9] The

journalist Emma Patterson is not convinced. Julia was a screen goddess, and to see her as a mother of three with "stomach sag-age" flaunt-
ing her wrinkly tum in front of us all is no way for a superstar to behave.
Patterson is disappointed: "She is a Hollywood icon and we all used to
aspire to her stunning looks, eagerly devouring the celeb pages for her
latest snaps. And this picture's kinda ruined that—just like the rest of
us mere, flawed mortals, she's not that pleasing picture of perfection we
so enjoyed looking at."[10] Having been given the case for against Julia's
mummy tummy, we are asked to make a decision and send our opinions
into the newspaper's Web pages. Julia may be an icon and a goddess or
even an ideal "real" mum, but ultimately her fate lies in our hands—or at
least we are led to think that this is the case.

Judgment in celebrity culture lies in the genre of melodrama,
which permeates the discourse. It creates community in a complex
way. Melodrama as a repertoire has references to the miserable and the
dramatic. It is sensational and also sentimental, but it has a particular
"moral undertone." "Life in the repertoire of melodrama becomes gro-
tesquely magnified. In the vale of tears that it is, celebrities play crucial and highly stereotyped roles, reminiscent of folk and oral culture."[11]
Melodrama comes into play when audiences are shocked and indignant;
it allows a space to process censure and disapproval of the actions of
individual celebrities. Thus, says Graeme Turner, "[c]elebrities become
the locations for the discussion and evaluation of the dramatic happen-
ings of everyday life: divorces, deaths, disappointments in career and so
on."[12] The sensationalism in the coverage of celebrity narratives is a key
aspect of their structure, but these elements are not designed to deliver
a "benign response." In fact, J. Hermes observes that these melodra-
matic characteristics made the respondents in her study feel better about
themselves. The misery of others somehow enabled individuals to cope
with their own lives in a different way.[13] Yet, she argues, "at the heart of
the repertoire of melodrama, there is also a deep sense that the world is
unjust, which points to a more collective sense of social inequality. To
enjoy it when things are going badly for 'rich and famous people' (as one
of my readers put it) is a way of imagining cosmic (rather than political)
justice taking its toll. Commiseration and indignation are equal ingredi-
ents of the pleasure of reading gossip magazines."[14]

The gossip column functions as a place where things are "set right." The columnist serves the interests of "justice in a corrupt world."[15] The tabloid treatment of celebrity culture is not so much concerned with presenting a figure that we might admire as in exacting a kind of righteous revenge on privilege and wealth. The tabloids give "voice to the pent-up frustration and indignation at the excesses of those who have come from recognisably ordinary backgrounds and have "made it" in understandable ways."[16] The indignation is not against the fact of wealth or, indeed, the media processes that it celebrates; it is more a targeted resentment that these things have come to "them" and not to "us." This leads to complicated and nuanced judgments concerning particular celebrities and the reasons why they are undeserving or have squandered their talent. The judgments are made socially in conversation with others and in relation to the media coverage, and they form a key part of celebrity discourse.

Making judgments entails a kind of theological debate. The example of Julia's mummy tummy takes us directly into questions concerning Julia's symbolic significance. Is she the distant screen icon, or a symbol of down-to-earth real womanhood? This is in the same territory as Watson's discussion of the difference between celebrities who are like Unmade Beds and those who are Pristine Pillows. Theological and religious analogies are used with some frequency within these kinds of discussions. To speak of a screen goddess carries an irony and also a reference point. The reader is drawn into the conversation and asked to take a view. No one involved in this everyday aspect of celebrity culture would say that this was a discussion about "theology" or that it was religious. Yet the theological is there. It is invoked and it is made use of, and as a result its meaning starts to shift. The metaphors are dislocated from their usual context, and they develop new associations. So as theological themes are taken up in popular culture they are simultaneously disconnected from traditional frameworks of meaning and relocated in a dialogue concerning the sacred self.

Hello! Heaven

The daughters of Bruce Willis and Demi Moore have joined the European debutantes at the Crillon Ball in Paris. "I guess it's every

French girl's dream," said the seventeen-year-old Scout LaRue Willis. Demi was keen to emphasize the cultured nature of the event: "I'm really pleased that Scout has met all these lovely other women from around the world."[17] This is the vision of the high life and the good life that is presented each week in Europe's oldest celebrity magazine, *Hello!* Scout and her fellow debutantes, who include the daughters of Phil Collins, Kristin Scott Thomas, and Carrie Fisher, and the granddaughter of John F. Kennedy, are dressed in their ball gowns by the world's top fashion houses, and they are escorted to the ball by the young bucks of the European aristocracy.

This is *Hello!* heaven, a vision of the celebrity world that is glossy and ideal. *Hello!* magazine started in 1944 when the Spanish journalist Antonia Sanchez Gomez launched a new weekly magazine called *¡Hola!* With the first issue, which had a print run of 14,000 copies, Gomez had a "brainwave" and put a picture of Clark Gable on the cover. It sold out, and "[c]elebrity journalism, *¡Hola!/Hello!*-style, was born."[18] From the beginning, *Hello!* presented a mix of Hollywood stars and minor European royalty with an ample sprinkling of B-list, C-list, and D-list pop singers; TV presenters; and people who might be, will be, are at present, or were once married to someone who was kind of famous.

"*¡Hola!* was an odd little Spanish publication." says Borkowski, "covering its cranky Euro-royals, Count von This and Baroness von That, but it specialised in picture-driven stories. . . . *Hello!* arrived with perfect timing just when the collateral of celebrity was going through a change. It coincided with the rise of the big-cheese PR men, especially in California, who wanted copy-approval for interviews with their clients, who recognised how much the magazines needed them more than vice versa."[19] Walsh argues that the magazine has at its heart a significant paradox. On the one hand it is entirely focused on a world of wealth, fame, "fabulous success, deranged consumer spending and the expectation that romance will always be around the corner—everything, in short, that the world associates with happiness."[20] Unfortunately, the figures who live in this world, as we know, seem to spend most of their time "being unhappy, unwell, doomed to rehab clinics, socially maladroit, sexually incontinent and unable to look after their children, [and] it has been *Hello!* magazine's unenviable task to put a brave face, and a positive construction, on the slow-motion motorway crash of famous people's lives."[21]

Magazines like *Hello!* take us into the enchanted lives of the celebrities. We glimpse a privileged vision of the good life, the heavenly life of the gods. Film stars pose alongside the super rich and the aristocracy. There appear to be many rooms in the heavenly mansion, but some celebrities clearly have found a way to make sure that they occupy the penthouse suites and luxury villas. But while there may be a social hierarchy, we are reassured that it is not closed. *Hello!* heaven remains open to those who get a lucky break or manage to marry the sons of multimillionaires. We see the celebrities smiling and graciously allowing us a glimpse of their "wonderful homes." We see the original Tudor beams, the swimming pool in Beverly Hills, and the vineyard in the south of France. The good life, we are assured, delivers material rewards, yet the chief of these is a "home." Extravagant it may be, even venial, but it is the material that is linked to the relational. These are nests. Every picture shouts out loud, "Look at my success. My wealth has bought me this—a 'place' to be happy and to enjoy my family and friends." The good life, represented by the gods, demigods, and wannabe gods, is fundamentally about happy families.

FAITHFUL GODS

In January 2008, the *National Enquirer* was worried: David Duchovny was cheating on his wife, Angelina seemed to be having some kind of postnatal depression, and Mel Gibson appeared to have rather too much interest in a "brunette beauty caught in his movie trailer." The worries didn't stop there; it seemed that singer and actress Mandy Moore, who, less than two months after she split with the singer Ryan Adams, was now getting "hot and heavy" with actor André Vippolis; and Lindsay Lohan had said, "she means it, girls; Don't you DARE get femme-flirty when Sapphic squeeze SAMANTHA RONSON's spinning discs at a club or green-eyed Lilo will get your perky butt kicked OUT!"[22]

On the face of it these kinds of stories demonstrate a prurient interest in the private lives of the famous. There is an intrusive curiosity concerning infidelities and an ever-vigilant eye for the dysfunctional relationship. Yet there is also a deeper current that drives these stories, even as they pander to our more base curiosity: fidelity. We want our gods to be faithful. We are desperate for relationships to work. Of course there's not much of a story in fidelity, but we need it somehow. It is this complicated question of faithfulness that lies, for instance, behind the interest in the "love" triangle between Jennifer Aniston, Brad Pitt, and Angelina Jolie. Jennifer Aniston was the nation's favorite "friend." Millions of women copied the haircut made famous by the character Rachel, played by Aniston in the hit series *Friends*.[23] "Jen" was the girl next door, and she married the most handsome of Hollywood's leading men, Brad Pitt; but Brad was unfaithful. Eventually he started an affair with Angelina, who everyone said was the most beautiful woman in the world. Brad and Angelina became Brangelina and embarked on the creation of a huge gaggle of children, part by natural processes and part by adoption. Jen has a relationship with singer John Mayer, but the speculation does not go away: "Brangelina to Split" and "Brad and Jen Get Back Together" headlines proliferate. The energy that fuels the tabloid frenzy around these three people is quite a phenomenon. The interest is of course in the narrative, but the power of that story comes from the subtext. We see in the story of Jen, Brad, and Angelina a projection of what is possibly our "ultimate concern," faithfulness. If the gods represent the worship of the self, this is a self that wants relationship and yet is all the time struggling with what that means. Trying to make sense of fidelity and desire, wanting to be the best but failing to make it—celebrity culture plays out these issues time and time again. Our concerns are embodied in the celebrity gods, goddesses, and love rats, and that is why we care (well, actually some of us couldn't care less, and that is kind of OK as well).

HOLY FAMILIES

The interest in celebrity relationships is closely matched by our fascination with their children. The first photograph of a celebrity child is a big event. It is an "outing" of tabloid importance. Nicole Kidman, we are told, is taking a walkabout in a "Wintry Paris with Her Sunday Girl."[24] The event has clearly been staged for the photographers. Kidman hugs her five-month-old and continually kisses her. She tells a press conference, "The rhythm of my life has changed. In my teens and twenties I wanted to change the world. Now I want to keep telling beautiful stories, but a lot of me is about my family."[25] Being a parent is part of the good life. Celebrities want to be seen as devoted parents, caring for their offspring.

Following the mayhem of his marriage to Britney Spears, Kevin Federline is pictured with his two lovely children in his "Spanish-style" L.A. home with the swimming pool and kids' playhouse/climbing frame and swings. Federline has been granted custody of the children following his divorce from Britney. "Being a father is everything," he says. "It's probably the best experience of my life . . . I always knew I wanted to be a father. It's a part of life that I am grateful for."[26] Celebrity children signify the blessed life of those who are rich and famous. We are drawn to the children of celebrities in part because this is a new dimension of celebrity life for us to identify with. Yet celebrity children are also important because they represent the birth of potential gods and another life on which we can feast via the media.

Celebrity status is increasingly passed on from parent to child. So in the rock world we have Ziggy Marley, Stella McCartney, Jade Jagger, and Peaches Geldof. Members of the rock royalty seem to be able to establish celebrity dynasties, and so the children of the gods appear to be blessed with semidivine status. Incorporation into the heavenly families of celebrity, however, is increasingly taking place through adoption. The headline was predictable: "Madonna and Child." The headline wrote itself when Guy Ritchie and Madonna were planning to adopt an orphan from Malawi. David Banda was the first of two African children that Madonna adopted. Angelina Jolie and Brad Pitt have also adopted a number of children from developing countries. Jolie calls this her "rainbow" approach to families. "It's a very special thing," she said. "There's something about traveling somewhere and finding your family."[27] Jolie is not the first celebrity to adopt children from around the world. In the 1970s Mia Farrow raised a family of fourteen children, ten of whom were adopted, and from a previous celebrity world the blues singer Josephine Baker adopted a large number of children from different ethnic backgrounds. Baker wanted to show that despite their differences people could get along. Baker, like Jolie, called her family the "Rainbow Tribe."[28] Adoption seems to signify a desire to "rescue" the world one person at a time. It is the personal counterpart to campaigns to save the rain forest and cancel third world debt. By extending their families, the gods seem to be at work as saviors. The family as "salvation" connects to the desire for fidelity and the priority of the home (actually four homes, one in Martinique, one in New York, one in London, and a little place close to Bono and the Edge on the Côte D'Azur). These are the key themes in the worship of the sacred self.

APOTHEOSIS

Not everyone can be born into a celebrity family, and only a few are chosen for adoption, but there is one sure route that mortals can take to instant fame: the reality TV show. The real prize in reality TV, says Turner, is not so much the cash that is on offer but the chance to be on television for months.[29] Contestants take part in a show like *Big Brother* or *Survivor* not so they can demonstrate that they have any particular talent or skill but to ensure that they are on the screen long enough to become famous. As Kylie Minogue says, "Fame used to be a by-product. Now its [sic] like 'What do you want to be when you grow up?' 'Famous.' 'What for?' 'It doesn't matter.'"[30]

For Leo Braudy the contemporary pursuit of fame is understandable. Fame, he argues, offers not just visibility for the individual but a particular kind of visibility. In modern fame, all "blemishes are smoothed and all wounds healed." Fame delivers a kind of magical moment of perfection that restores "integrity and wholeness" to the self. To become famous in an arbitrary way is even more beneficial and supportive of the sense of individuality: "To be famous for yourself, for what you are without talent or premeditation, means you have come into your rightful inheritance." This sort of fame, says Braudy, is a self-justification.[31] For others, exposure of the self on television is to occupy a position in the public sphere. Access to the media means the ability to be present in the central social space in our culture. The disclosure of the self therefore is less a cult of personal narcissism than an attempt to find a voice or a position in the new form of democratic platform.[32]

In the 1970s Blondie cheerfully recommended that we should "Die Young Stay Pretty."[33] Thankfully Debbie Harry didn't heed her own advice, but then neither has Pete Townshend fulfilled his own wish to die before he gets old; premature death is nevertheless one of the main ways that celebrities achieve a semidivine status. Actually it is not just death, it is death plus the ability to leave a product that can be reproduced and sold. So Elvis' voice and image can be endlessly circulated. The same is true of James Dean, Jimi Hendrix, and John Lennon. Interestingly, this is less true for a figure such as Jade Goody, whose "product" was the unfolding drama of her life and eventually her death. It is the media that make gods, and it is the media that ensure that our gods are immortal. Immortality means that your movie is playing somewhere, your image is on a T-shirt, and someone is finding a way to make some money from you even when you are dead.

REVELATION

It is a routine magazine interview. Will Smith is turning forty. In *Touch* wants to know how Will is doing with this. In typical joking style, he responds, "I'm turning 40 this year, so I'm going to be naked as much as possible before it's too late."[34] Right next to the interview is a picture of the star coming out of the sea wearing a pair of swimming trunks. Will clearly works out, he's in great shape. The picture carries an inset comment: "He's comfortable with his body." But Will says, "I've never seen myself as sexy."[35] So it is not just his honed torso that is revealed, we are seemingly let into the star's inner thoughts. He doesn't see himself as sexy. This is the first of a series of revelations. Will tells us that he has learned that money does not make you happy but that since the first day he heard his voice on the radio singing a song he had written he has felt that his life has been "beyond everything that I ever dreamed."[36] Will starts the interview by talking about his children. Now that he is forty, he says, he is telling them they must listen to him. Problem is that they don't. *In Touch* wants to know, how does he balance his work and his family? Will says it is one of the benefits of his job that he can include his kids, but now that they are older they are less keen to hang out with Mommy and Daddy. Will tells us that the kids are homeschooled, and it is one of his ambitions to "open a real school."[37] It is only in the last question that we get a mention of the movie *Hancock*—this is the "product" that Will is promoting, and it is the reason for the interview.

Baring the flesh and sharing with us a photo of his family, Will plays the celebrity game of "revelation." The real commodity is not this particular movie (which seems to have died at the box office) but Will himself. It is this wholesome family image that sells the movie, not the other way round. Tennis champion Boris Becker doesn't have a movie to promote, but on the eve of the Wimbledon Championships it seems that he has been signed up by the fashion house Ralph Lauren. The magazine cuts right to the chase. Boris of course is a legendary tennis player, but what we all know about him is that he had what the magazine tactfully calls "a hasty encounter" with the Russian model Angela Ermakova in a London restaurant (rather implausibly but nevertheless intriguingly, at the time it was reported that the dirty deed was done in a cupboard in the dining room). After a lengthy court case and a DNA test, Boris was forced to accept the paternity of a daughter. Boris, we are now reassured, provides both mother and daughter with an apartment in central London.[38] The good news, depending on how you see these things, is that Boris, it seems, is now single again, having split up with his girlfriend, the model Sharlely Kerssenberg, but he is also a "contented family man." Said Boris, "The first month or two without a girlfriend was difficult but now I don't miss it. I did have some long nights but age is a great healer. I just had another glass of red wine, fell asleep and woke up."[39] At one time Boris earned his living as one of the greatest tennis players in the world. Now he sells himself. This is the celebrity currency of revelation.

In 2004 MTV launched the groundbreaking reality TV show *The Osbournes*. The show took us into the home of the rock star Ozzy Osbourne and chronicled the antics of his family. Over a three-year period viewers got to know Ozzy's powerful wife Sharon, along with his rebellious daughter Kelly and ever-troubled son Jack. The show became MTV's highest-rated series, with an audience of 7.8 million in the U.S. alone. The series ensured that Kelly and Jack could make a seamless and highly profitable move from Beverly Hills high school brats to media celebs. Ozzy seemed to transition from slightly obscure rock god who had a predilection for biting the heads off bats into a British national treasure who was deemed worthy of performing at Buckingham Palace in front of the Queen and other members of the Royal Family. Sharon Osbourne, meanwhile, has become a media sensation as a judge on the hit series *America's Got Talent*.

The celebrity reality show and the personal interview are the energizing substance of celebrity worship. They take us into the personality and the private world of the star. They offer a nuanced and "real" picture of a life. It is this revelation of life that facilitates worship and identification. Through the processes of revelation, the celebrities offer themselves up for consumption. Sharon Osbourne's Web site is up front about this, stating, "Here's a woman who's all about empowerment, without any of the tokenistic acknowledgment of females that usually lurks behind that phrase. That's human empowerment, as in not taking no for answer, never taking any of life's mess lying down, and recognising tall brick walls but simply driving around them."[40] We know that this is true because we beheld the image, we saw the show, and it was good.

INCARNATION

Celebrity gods are embodied divinities. Worship is focused on the celebration of their perfect forms. Magazines parade celebrities in various kinds of undress. We are treated to beach pictures in which guys show off their honed chests as they run in and out of the sea and throw footballs to one another. *Star* magazine is impressed with actor Kiefer Sutherland, who at forty-one is in "awesome shape," and chef Gordon Ramsay, we are told, is "surprisingly buff."[41] The perfect body is more than an aesthetic appreciation. This is about sex. Celebrities are the objectivization of desire, and sex is the link between the star system and psychoanalysis: "Both [the star system and psychoanalysis] take identity (or even personality) as their object: both depend upon a model of surface and depth and search for the true identity beneath surface manifestations; both look to a private, familial identity to locate that truth, and both assume, furthermore, that the truth, is at its core, sexual."[42] The body signifies the divine self, and in celebrity culture this divine self is sexual.

The self, sex, and the body are an obsessive preoccupation, and as a result keeping in shape is a constant theme. Keeping in shape articulates the body and identity. Keeping in shape signifies that celebrities are "making the most of themselves." Working out equals working on the self as a locus of the sacred. Nowhere is this pressure to maintain the self more evident than when a celebrity has just had a baby. A good example of this comes from a Hollywood gossip blog. The writer is deeply impressed with

Nicole Richie, who is clearly making an effort: "Less than a month after giving birth to her second child. Nicole Richie has the balls to step out in a clingy romper on a date night with her baby's daddy Joel Madden. This *baby bounce back* is even fast by Hollywood standards. Expect to see Sara Michelle Gellar stepping out in skinny jeans very soon. In L.A. losing baby weight is more competitive than the freakin' Olympics."[43] Staying in shape is more than a competition—it signifies the will to perfection, the fulfillment of the self. Those celebrities who start to look out of shape are only worthy of our disdain. They are gods who don't seem to be making an effort. They are falling down on the job.

Sin

Celebrity coverage does not fight shy of the idea of sin. In fact, sin and different kinds of wrongdoing form a great deal of the content of celebrity narratives. Interestingly, celebrities themselves may even acknowledge their own faults in very public ways. In December 2009, the golfer Tiger Woods made a public confession of his "sins" on his Web site. Following a bizarre incident the previous month when he crashed his car into a fire hydrant outside his home in Florida, allegations of a string of extramarital affairs started to emerge in the press.[44] This prompted Woods to issue the following statement: "I have let my family down and I regret those transgressions with all of my heart. I have not been true to my values and the behavior my family deserves. I am not without faults and I am far short of perfect. I am dealing with my behavior and personal failings behind closed doors with my family. Those feelings should be shared by us alone."[45]

Sports heroes, says Turner, carry a weight of expectation that would never apply to figures such as Ozzy Osbourne or Jack Nicholson.[46] The sports star as a role model has a long history. Sports stars represent the nation "formally" when they appear for the national team. To be a successful sportsman or sportswoman it is not simply enough, says Turner, to perform well on the pitch or in the pool or on the course. Performance extends to the personal and private spheres of a sports star's life. According to Turner, it is common for sports stars to be reminded of their responsibilities as role models. Once sports stars have been perceived to have let the fans (and indeed in some cases the country) down, the media are very happy to rebuke them.[47] Tiger Woods appears to have internalized, to a significant extent, the high expectations of his fans. His statement shows a person in crisis, but it also reveals something of the understanding of "sin" in popular culture. Sin relates to "personal values" and letting down those you love. The moral imperative here does not come from any external morality or commandment, rather it comes from being true to the best of your self. Letting yourself down becomes the framework for understanding not only wrongdoing but also more general failure to achieve. Celebrity sin gathers energy from the perception that the stars have everything going for them but somehow they have messed up. Tiger had a beautiful wife, he was on the way to being the undisputed greatest golfer of all time, and he was a friend of the president of the United States. His public "transgression" was a fall from a very great height. Celebrities seem to be particularly prone to this kind of moral collapse.

Just following the incredible success of the film *Four Weddings and a Funeral* and when he was still in a relationship with model Elizabeth Hurley, the actor Hugh Grant was arrested in Hollywood for inviting a prostitute to join him in his car. After the arrest, Grant was reported to have said, "I did something completely insane. I have hurt people I love and embarrassed people I work with. For both things I am more sorry than I can say."[48] Three years after Grant's arrest in Hollywood, the pop singer George Michael was also arrested in Beverly Hills for "lewd behavior" in a public place. Four years after the event (and several scrapes with the law and tabloids later), Michael spoke publicly about the incident. He said that at the time he was dealing with the death of his mother and that of his former partner, Anselmo Feleppa: "I think, with hindsight, I did it to myself and I tried to work out why. And suddenly, it was a way of making my life about me. And for six months it worked."[49] In celebrity culture, "sin" is not only acknowledged, it is often confessed in public. Transgression, however, is linked to a narrative of the self. To sin is to fail to be the best that you can be. Sin is ultimately about "me."

THE WAGES OF SIN IS "MELTDOWN"

In 2008 headlines in the press reported on another Britney Spears "meltdown."[50] The young singer, who had been a child star at the age of eleven on *The Mickey Mouse Club*, had been through a series of relationship breakdowns following her meteoric rise to pop stardom. Britney was the all-American girl who proclaimed her virginity and wore a convent uniform, pigtails, and a suggestive pout while singing, "Hit me baby one more time." "She brought back softness and femininity and all-American girlhood," says Caroline Lettieri, "but she wrapped it up with lashings of sex. It was very clever, great fun, a big tease, kind of an outrage, and, boy, did it sell records."[51] The reporting of Britney's subsequent troubles was brutal: "The career is shot, the looks have gone, the marriage is over, the children have been taken away. Under 24-hour suicide watch in a Los Angeles hospital until her release on Saturday night, Britney Spears, the pop princess turned human train wreck, cuts a pathetic, lost and strangely reproachful figure."[52] "Meltdown" is a telling phrase, as if the "image" of the star was formed from wax or shaped from ice. The celebrity as typified by Britney Spears is magnificent but ultimately a fragile construct.

Falling short, failing to live up to the ideal, is always carried in the body in celebrity culture. Sin is somatized. Chris Rojek calls this the "mortification of the body." "Descent," Rojek says, "is established by routines of behaviour that centre on the mortification of the body. Thus, celebrities may become anorexic, or balloon in weight, develop phobias about being in public places, succumb to narcotic addiction or engage in public displays of drunkenness."[53] We see our gods in crisis. They stumble even as they are on the red carpet. Just as they carry their divinity in their perfect skin, they similarly manifest their mortality. They are flesh and blood, just like us. Actually, they are probably not just like us, because given the opportunity we wouldn't throw it all away like they seem to do, but maybe this is the behavior of gods. They burn brightly, but they do not last.

The celebrity star's pattern of elevation and dramatic fall echoes mythic notions of the dying and rising god.[54] Britney's media story is structured around this pattern. We alternately see her buildup and celebration as the teenage pop sensation, and then we see her demise and fall. This story is repeated over and over again with celebrities from Marilyn Monroe and Judy Garland through to Amy Winehouse. Resurrection, however, is always a possibility. We enjoy seeing our gods rise again. The new album, the critically acclaimed part in a movie, or the TV soap part is just around the corner. But resurrection is in some cases not possible. In celebrity culture there is such a thing as the unforgivable sin. This sin involves the harming of others. So while some may pass through tragedy and return to a similar popularity, for figures such as O. J. Simpson or Gary Glitter it seems that there is no return.

REDEMPTION (REHAB)

Celebrities generally find it quite a routine matter to turn their lives around. More often than not, redemption equals a spell in rehab. In 2005 the supermodel Kate Moss was embroiled in a drugs scandal. Kate was pictured at a recording studio with her then boyfriend, himself a notorious drug addict, Pete Doherty from the band Babyshambles. Journalist Stephen Moyes of the *Daily Mirror* describes the scene witnessed by the newspaper's undercover reporter: "As the white powder induces a sudden rush to her brain, she rocks back in her seat and laughs hysterically. The coke is kicking in. Within seconds she leans forward and again sniffs into a tightly rolled-up £5 note, hoovering up every last grain of the Class A drug." Moyes concludes that Kate must be a practiced user.[55] When the story broke, Kate lost a significant number of modeling contracts. Her response was to check into the Meadows Clinic in Arizona. There her "therapy" was reported to have lasted around a month. When she left the clinic, she was said to have been looking forward to getting back to work.[56] Rehab worked for Kate, and her redemption was confirmed when she landed an estimated £12 million worth of deals with Longchamp, Roberto Cavalli, and Calvin Klein.[57] Celebrity redemption, it seems, is the ultimate prosperity gospel, where salvation is measured by the bottom line.

Martha Stewart's redemption is even more remarkable than that of Kate Moss. Stewart, says Cashmore, is Delia Smith crossed with Dame Judi Dench with the affection from the public normally reserved for Mother Teresa. In 2004 Stewart was found guilty of illegal dealings in stocks and shares, and she served twelve months in prison. When she walked out of jail, however, her company had tripled in value, and she was quickly offered a high-profile role on the television show *The Apprentice*.[58] Cashmore sees the Stewart story as one of "fall and redemption." He quotes Robert Wright, the CEO of Universal, defending the use of Stewart in the reality television competition as saying that "Americans are waiting for the next act. They want to see a happy ending."

SAVIORS

In the celebrity world, some figures seem to play the role of savior. They take it upon themselves to rescue stars who are going through hard times. A good example of this is Sir Elton John. In 1997 Elton was said to have "kidnapped" the singer Robbie Williams and forced Robbie to confront his problems with drugs and alcohol. Robbie later told how Elton drove him to a clinic: "I was sandwiched by two people in the back of the car, so I wouldn't try to commit suicide or run off."[59] Writing in 2009, the journalist Marina Hyde reported that the troubled singer George Michael was well aware of Elton's savior complex but that George was determined not to be saved. George was very clear that he did not want this kind of attention: "He will not be happy until I bang on his door in the middle of the night saying, 'Please, please, help me, Elton. Take me to rehab.' It's not going to happen. You know what I heard last week? That Bono . . . Oh for God's sake . . ." He's choking on his laughter. "Geri [Halliwell] told Kenny that Bono, having spoken to Elton, had approached Geri to say, 'What can we do for George?'"[60]

Celebrities don't just save one another, increasingly they are turning their savior complexes toward the wider world. Bob Geldof is the archetype of the celebrity who is a politician "without office."[61] Geldof was "reincarnated as St Bob when he organized the global Live Aid Concert in 1985," says Cashmore.[62] The Live Aid concert raised $100 million, which made it by far the largest single charity event that has taken place. Says Cashmore, "So effective was the mass action that it announced the arrival of rock stars and other celebrities in global politics."[63] Rock musicians have been particularly drawn to develop messiah complexes. From Bob Dylan on through to R.E.M., U2, and now Coldplay, musicians have sought to mobilize opinion and influence world events.[64] Actors have also been engaged politically, says Cashmore, with figures such as Jane Fonda, Barbra Streisand, Susan Sarandon, and Woody Harrelson prominent among Hollywood campaigners.[65] Celebrities are more and more inclined to endorse charities. An example, says Cashmore, is Coldplay's support for Oxfam's Make Trade Fair campaign.[66] Through their involvement with charities, celebrities may be seen as "navigational aids."[67] Charities such as Oxfam use celebrities because they manage to convert "very complex economic and political arguments . . . into digestible and easily understandable chunks of information that will fit into the contexts of media viewing."[68]

In 1976 Bob Marley played in front of a crowd of 80,000 people in his native Jamaica. Jamaican politics had been mired in a series of violent confrontations between opposing parties. At the climax of the concert, Marley called onto the stage the prime minister of Jamaica, Michael Manley, and the opposition leader, Edward Seaga. In a powerful symbolic gesture calling for reconciliation, the singer joined the hands of these two leaders together and held them above his head.[69] For the music writer Robert Palmer, Bob Marley is one of the most significant figures in the history of rock music: "No one in rock and roll has left a musical legacy that matters more or one that matters in such fundamental ways," said Palmer.[70] Marley is not simply important because of his impact on the politics of Jamaica, arguably he also has a powerful religious significance: "In the two decades since Bob Marley has gone, it is clear that he is without question one of the most transcendent figures of the past hundred years. The ripples of his unparalleled achievements radiate outward through the river of his music into an ocean of politics, ethics, fashion, philosophy and religion. His story is a timeless myth made manifest in this way, right before our disbelieving eyes."[71]

Oprah Winfrey represents a more personal salvation that that of Bob Geldof or Bob Marley. Oprah is the voice of "women in the middle."[72] She represents women who are working to be something in their over-full lives: "These women are trying to manage busy lives and households, address personal and social concerns, and maybe also lose some weight."[73] Oprah Winfrey's message is clear, "Live your best life."[74] Oprah offers tools to enable her viewers to achieve this goal. She produces books to read and people to emulate and an assortment of products to help the public to live their best life. Oprah may not be a pastor, but she offers pastoral care.[75] But Oprah wants not only to "fix individuals" but also to fix whole communities. She is a noted philanthropist, with interests in a range of charitable projects, including The

Oprah Winfrey Foundation and Oprah's Angel Network. *BusinessWeek* reported that over her lifetime Oprah will have given away up to 13 percent of her estimated $1.3 billion net worth.[76] Oprah is popular not simply with black audiences, she is particularly popular with whites. It helps that Oprah represents a familiar archetype: "She is the good black mama who takes care of white kids."[77] Oprah locates individual betterment within the context of communal betterment. Her "attempt to transform community by promoting individual transformation is also a way of placing individuals within a wider community."[78]

THE SPIRIT

Celebrities are very often religious, or at least they represent themselves as being, to a greater or lesser extent, spiritual. For Oprah Winfrey, spirituality is what emerges from experience. Oprah "talks out of experience and relates to people talking out of experience. Spirituality talk is talk that arises out of experience."[79] So Oprah may be a chat show host, but she does not peddle talk for talk's sake: "It is not just talk, but talk that's been tested in life's fires—talk as testimony."[80] This kind of talk is the "language of authenticity"—it represents the vitality of experience as opposed to the dryness of religious institution.[81] Oprah speaks about values; these are the things that are important for her, and she believes they are important for her audience. She is not a "religious figure," but her values are rooted in a religious tradition: "Oprah has transformed herself and what she is doing in a series of makeovers over time, and yet there is a core of consistency in what she does. She has made herself into an exemplar of values, a shaper of tastes, and an entertainer."[82] Oprah transforms what religions call "transcendence" into something that is secular and inspiring.

Celebrities seem to embrace a variety of different religions. In 1964 the boxer Cassius Clay converted to become a follower of the Nation of Islam. He changed his name to Muhammad Ali to symbolize this conversion. For the next ten years, until he converted to orthodox Islam, Ali was the most prominent supporter of the Nation of Islam.[83] Madonna is known as an enthusiastic advocate of the Jewish sect Kabbalah. She was introduced to the group through the actress Sandra Bernhard and ever since has been an evangelist for the cause, with Lindsay Lohan being among her celebrity converts.[84] In 2008 a video appeared on the Internet showing Tom Cruise talking about his belief in Scientology. Cruise speaks about his desire to spread the message of Scientology: "We are the authorities on getting people off drugs, we are the authorities on the mind, we are the authorities on improving conditions . . . [W]e can rehabilitate criminals . . . [W]e can bring peace and unite communities."[85] Muhammad Ali is seen as heroic, but Madonna's belief in Kabbalah is often reported with some incredulity, and Cruise's advocacy of Scientology is seen as baffling. The same could be said for Mel Gibson's ultra-Catholic beliefs, or indeed about the evangelical Christianity of a great many stars. Celebrity culture is tolerant of spirituality but skeptical of any kind of formal religious belief. We want our gods to be spiritual, but we do not want them to be inflexible or exclusivist in their advocacy of religion. And more than anything we really don't want them to turn into evangelists.

THEOLOGICAL MUTATIONS IN CELEBRITY CULTURE

The articulation of religious analogies in celebrity culture generates new and unexpected theological meaning. At its heart, celebrity culture facilitates the negotiation of the self through processes of representation, identification, and disidentification. The sacred, mixed in with a good dose of the profane, is taken up in this contested sphere. The religious is therefore (unwittingly) connected up with an ongoing dialogue about the possibilities of the self and how identity is to be formed and maintained in contemporary Western culture. This is an aspect of the subjective turn in religion.[86] Celebrity culture, however, is not a traditional "religion," it is a "sort of" religion or a para-religion. The theological operates primarily at the level of representation, and it only has an indirect purchase on the way that meaning is made in relation to celebrity discourses. Nevertheless, as analogy the theological is present in celebrity narratives, and it forms part of the symbolic world that operates as a reference point for identity formation. It is in this context that through articulation theological metaphors are subject to reformulation and mutation.

A number of theological themes have emerged from this survey of celebrity discourse. First and perhaps most significantly, the "sacred" is connected up with concerns about home, family, and relationships. While it may appear that celebrity culture is overly obsessed with infidelity, obscene wealth, and vulgar display, behind these preoccupations there are more enduring and surprisingly "moral" values in play. We desperately want our gods to be people who fall in love, have nice homes, and have beautiful children. We are not very concerned if the celebrity is gay, lesbian, or heterosexual, we just want, in fact we expect, him or her to stay faithful. This longing for relationship is mediated in and through the trappings of success. Material wealth and the good life are connected up with this deep and rich vein in celebrity culture. Celebrity gods, despite all appearances, seem to be situated in a rather wholesome frame of reference.

Similarly, the obsession with the body and its various delights is not entirely to do with voyeurism. We are not just gazing upon perfect (or slightly less than perfect) bodies. We like our idols to have godlike pecs and bodies that defy both age and gravity not simply because we can look at them but because it shows that celebrities "care." The body in this sense becomes a moral site. Godliness is incarnated, it is robed in flesh. At the same time, failure and sin are also carried in the body. We follow our gods to see if they have eating problems. We want to know if they have managed to overcome the birth of a child. Have they managed to find a way to stave off the march of time? Are they really immortal? Let's just check: have they got wrinkles, is there a trace of cellulite? These observations have energy because they demonstrate the extent to which our gods are "making the most of themselves." A strict moral imperative is operating in all of these kinds of conversations. In the religion of the sacred self, it is a sin to not make an effort.

The yearning for faithfulness and happy families and the sense that we should "make the most of ourselves" gives a shape to judgment and retribution in celebrity culture. This element in celebrity "theology" is also rather unexpected. The tabloids and various celebrity media seem to revel in fleshly wrongdoing. There is a pleasure in the prurient, but at root the reference point is not solely titillation. The real energy in celebrity coverage is the naming and shaming of sin. A kind of catharsis arises from wrongdoing in celebrity narratives. We are simultaneously drawn toward the knowledge of good and the knowledge of evil. We want details. We enjoy seeing our gods bite into the fruit, and we stick around to witness the juices running down their cheeks, but as we gaze on them we also judge. Sin in celebrity culture takes us into the troubled world of the religion of the self. We are conflicted, twisted, and generally confused not only by our own wrongdoing but by that of others.

In celebrity culture, "everyone deserves a second chance." Redemption is always possible. We accept that our gods will mess up. Everyone makes mistakes; after all, they are only human. Redemption, however, does not come from any external savior or divine force. In the religion of the sacred self we are expected to "turn ourselves around." Salvation may come very quickly through a stay in rehab or a heartrending interview on a chat show, but it is always material. The interviews and the rehab help, as will an overt and public effort to support a charity, but these are nothing if they are not accompanied by product. The redeemed need to show that they have repented by parading the hot new album, the brilliant performance in a blockbuster movie, or the lucrative advertising contract. Saint (Elton) John says that sorry is the "hardest word," but it cuts very little ice if it is not backed up by tangible evidence of the redeemed life.

And Finally a Word from Our Sponsors

Celebrity culture is a ubiquitous and spreading phenomenon. It has infiltrated most if not all aspects of life. From sports and politics to entertainment and economics, the celebrity has become a key building block in the way that the media present and interpret life. In the media and in common parlance, celebrities are routinely associated with religion. The relationships that individuals form with celebrities are often seen as a kind of religious adoration. Yet celebrity worship is not a "religion" in the formal sense. It is a "kind of" religion or a para-religion. This para-religion offers an insight into the way that the religious or the theological persists in media representation. This approach to celebrity culture as a form of religion in this sense sits alongside the developing field of religion, media, and popular culture. What it contributes, however, is an insight into celebrity as an involving or participating para-religious culture. Celebrities get under our skin. We are prompted to take a view and make a judgment. In this sense celebrity culture as a form of para-religion is different than, say, religion in film or in popular music. It is trashier, but it is at the same time more provocative. It is this ability to irritate and to generate moral judgment that fuels the specifically religious or theological innovations that make up celebrity culture. For as theological themes are incorporated into this discourse of the meaning(less) in celebrity worship, they are subject to change. These changes are a clue to the future of religion in contemporary culture, both for ill and for good.

NOTES

INTRODUCTION

1   For examples of religion in media and popular culture, see Robert K. Johnson, *Reel Spirituality: Theology and Film in Dialogue* (Grand Rapids, Mich.: Baker Books, 2000); Lynn Schofield Clark, *From Angels to Aliens: Teenagers, the Media, and the Supernatural* (Oxford: Oxford University Press, 2003); Robin Sylvan, *Traces of the Spirit: The Religious Dimensions of Popular Music* (New York: New York University Press, 2002); James B. Twitchell, *Adcult USA: The Triumph of Advertising in American Culture* (New York: Columbia University Press, 1996); and Diane Winston, ed., *Small Screen, Big Picture: Television and Lived Religion* (Waco, Tex.: Baylor University Press, 2009).

2   Malcolm Boyd, *Christ and Celebrity Gods* (Greenwich, Conn.: Seabury Press, 1958).

3   Boyd, *Christ*, 8.

4   Boyd, *Christ*, 11, 12.

5   Gary Laderman, *Sacred Matters: Celebrity Worship, Sexual Ecstasies, the Living Dead, and Other Signs of Religious Life in the United States* (New York: New Press, 2009), 64, 65.

6   Laderman, *Sacred*, 71.

7   Ian Bradley, *You've Got to Have a Dream: The Message of the Musical* (London: SCM Press, 2004), 19.

8   Paul Heelas and Linda Woodhead, *The Spiritual Revolution: Why Religion Is Giving Way to Spirituality* (Oxford: Blackwell, 2005), 2.

CHAPTER 1

1   Maggie Shiels, "Web Slows after Jackson's Death," BBC News, June 26, 2009, http://news.bbc.co.uk/1/hi/8120324.stm.
2   Mary Hockaday, "Michael Jackson Coverage," BBC News, June 29, 2009, http://www.bbc.co.uk/blogs/theeditors/2009/06/michael_jackson_coverage.html.
3   Urmee Khan, "BBC Criticised Over Jade Goody Coverage," *Daily Telegraph*, March 25, 2009, http://www.telegraph.co.uk/news/newstopics/celebritynews/jade-goody/5045083/BBC-criticised-over-Jade-Goody-coverage.html.
4   Stuart Jeffries, "Obituary: Jade Goody," *Guardian*, March 22, 2009, http://www.guardian.co.uk/media/2009/mar/22/jade-goody-obituary.
5   Stephen Glover, "Stephen Glover: This Celebration of Ordinariness by the Media Leaves Me Bemused," *Independent*, February 23, 2009, http://www.independent.co.uk/news/media/opinion/stephen-glover/stephen-glover-this-celebration-of-ordinariness-by-the-media-leaves-me-bemused-1629289.html.
6   "Actor Heath Ledger Dies at 28," CNN.com/entertainment, January 22, 2008, http://edition.cnn.com/2008/SHOWBIZ/Movies/01/22/heath.ledger.dead/index.html.
7   http://celebsinside.com/2008/01/25/heath-ledger-fans-mourn/.
8   Monica Guzman, "Cobain's Legacy Still Evolving 15 Years after Suicide," *Seattle Post-Intelligencer*, April 8, 2009, http://www.seattlepi.com/pop/404942_cobain08.html.
9   Guzman, "Cobain's Legacy."
10   Kathleen Crislip, "Tokens on Jim Morrison's Grave, Pere Lachaise Cemetery," About.com, 2006, http://studenttravel.about.com/od/eftoursphotos/ig/Pere-Lachaise-Paris-Cemetery/morris_plach_ef_06.htm.
11   "Marc Bolan's Rock Shrine," The Shady Old Lady's Guide to London, http://www.shadyoldlady.com/location.php?loc=373.
12   "Suge Knight and Many More on 2Pac's Death," AllEyezonMe.com, September 20, 1996, http://www.alleyezonme.com/2pacinterviews/tupacshakur/16/Suge_Knight_Interview.html.
13   R. B. Riddle, "The Man Tupac Amaru Shakur Remembered,"

HELLOarticle.com, http://www.helloarticle.com/the-man-tupac-amaru-shakur-remembered-r3182.htm.

14   Mitch Weiss quoted in Tom Brook, "The Night Lennon Died," BBC News, December 8, 2000, http://news.bbc.co.uk/1/hi/entertainment/1060306.stm.

15   Brook, "Lennon."

16   Laderman, *Sacred*, 65–69.

17   Laderman, *Sacred*, 68.

18   Jack O'Sullivan quoted in Paul Heelas, "Diana's Self and the Quest Within," in *Diana: The Making of a Media Saint*, ed. Jeffrey Richards, Scott Wilson, and Linda Woodhead (London: I. B. Tauris, 1999), 112.

19   O'Sullivan quoted in Heelas, "Diana's Self," 112.

20   Ian Jack quoted in Richards, Wilson, and Woodhead, *Diana*, 7.

21   Richards, Wilson, and Woodhead, *Diana*, 9.

22   George Carey quoted from Heelas, "Diana's Self," in Richards, Wilson, and Woodhead, *Diana*, 112.

23   Richards, Wilson, and Woodhead, *Diana*, 2.

24   Judith Williamson, "A Glimpse of the Void," in *After Diana: Irreverent Elegies*, ed. Mandy Merck (London: Verso, 1998), 27.

25   Williamson, "Glimpse," 26.

26   Williamson, "Glimpse," 26.

27   Camille Paglia, *Vamps and Tramps: New Essays* (London: Penguin Books, 1994), 164.

28   Paglia, *Vamps*, 166.

29   Paglia, *Vamps*, 168.

30   Cooper Lawrence, *The Cult of Celebrity: What Our Fascination with the Stars Reveals about Us* (Guilford, Conn.: Skirt, 2009), 4.

31   Bryan Robinson, "Why Are Michael Jackson's Fans So Devoted?" ABC News/Entertainment, February 23, 2005, http://abcnews.go.com/Entertainment/LegalCenter/Story?id=464753&page=2Fans.

32   Ibrahim Ramey, "Reflections on the Death of Michael Jackson, and the Worship of Celebrities," The Fellowship of Reconciliation, June 26, 2009. Originally posted at http://www.forpeace.net/blog/ibrahim-ramey/reflections-death-michael-jackson-and-worship-celebrities; now posted at http://forusa.org/blogs/ibrahim-ramey/reflections-death-michael-jackson-and-worship-celebrities.

33   SLyvetteRob, comment on "So Do We All Have Celebrity Worship

Syndrome? Lol," The MJFC Michael Jackson Fan Club, comment posted September 2, 2009, http://www.mjfanclub.net/mjforum373/showthread.php?t=13261.

34　Chris Rojek, *Celebrity* (London: Reaktion Books, 2001), 53.

35　Rojek, *Celebrity*, 57.

36　Rojek, *Celebrity*, 97.

37　Rojek, *Celebrity*, 57.

38　Rojek, *Celebrity*, 99.

39　Rojek, *Celebrity*, 99.

40　Lynn E. McCutcheon, Rense Lange, and James Houran, "Conceptualization and Measurement of Celebrity Worship," *The British Journal of Psychology* 93 (2002): 69.

41　McCutcheon, Lange, and Houran, "Conceptualization," 69.

42　McCutcheon, Lange, and Houran, "Conceptualization," 75.

43　McCutcheon, Lange, and Houran, "Conceptualization," 81.

44　John Maltby, Liza Day, Lynn E. McCutcheon, Raphael Gillett, James Houran, and Diane D. Ashe, "Personality and Coping: A Context for Examining Celebrity Worship and Mental Health," *The British Journal of Psychology* 95 (2004): 411–28.

45　John Maltby, David C. Giles, Louise Barber, and Lynn E. McCutcheon, "Intense-Personal Celebrity Worship and Body Image: Evidence of a Link among Female Adolescents," *The British Journal of Health Psychology* 10 (2005): 17–32.

46　Edgar Morin, *The Stars*, trans. Richard Howard (Minneapolis: University of Minnesota Press, 2005), 57. First published 1972.

47　Roland Barthes, *Mythologies*, trans. Annette Lavers (London: Paladin Books, 1972), 57. First published 1957.

48　Morin, *Stars*, 57.

49　Morin, *Stars*, 60.

50　Morin, *Stars*, 73.

51　Ellis Cashmore, *Celebrity/Culture* (Abingdon: Routledge, 2006), 79.

52　Cashmore, *Celebrity*, 79.

53　Reported in "Religious Nuts Worship Michael Jackson," CelebrityFIX, ninemsn.com, http://celebrities.ninemsn.com.au/?blogentryid=360412&showcomments=true.

54　"Religious Nuts," CelebrityFIX, ninemsn.com.

55　"Religious Nuts," CelebrityFIX, ninemsn.com.

56　Erika Doss, *Elvis Culture: Fans, Faith, and Image* (Lawrence: University Press of Kansas, 1999), 31.

57　Doss, *Elvis*, 77.

58　Doss, *Elvis*, 35.

59   Marylouise Caldwell and Paul Henry, "Living Dolls: How Affinity Groups Sustain Celebrity Worship" (presented at the 2009 Association for Consumer Research [ACR] Asia-Pacific Conference, Hyderabad, India, January 4, 2009, http://neumann.hec.ca/aimac2005/PDF_Text/CaldwellM_HenryP.pdf).
60   Caldwell and Henry, "Living," 7.
61   Caldwell and Henry, "Living," 7.
62   Doss, *Elvis*, 97.
63   Cashmore, *Celebrity*, 39.
64   Cashmore, *Celebrity*, 39.
65   Graeme Turner, *Understanding Celebrity* (London: Sage, 2004), 92.
66   Rojek, *Celebrity*, 52.
67   Rojek, *Celebrity*, 53.
68   Turner, *Understanding*, 23.
69   Turner, *Understanding*, 24.
70   Cashmore, *Celebrity*, 39.
71   Cashmore, *Celebrity*, 80.
72   Cashmore, *Celebrity*, 80.
73   Turner, *Understanding*, 102.
74   Turner, *Understanding*, 102.
75   Turner, *Understanding*, 102.
76   Alperstein quoted in Cashmore, *Celebrity*, 82.
77   Fraser and Brown quoted in Cashmore, *Celebrity*, 82.
78   Sandvoss quoted in Cashmore, *Celebrity*, 182.
79   Joshua Gamson, *Claims to Fame: Celebrity in Contemporary America* (Berkeley: University of California Press, 1994), 173.
80   Gamson, *Claims*, 173.
81   Gamson, *Claims*, 141.
82   John Frow, "Is Elvis a God? Cult, Culture, Questions of Method," *International Journal of Cultural Studies* 1, no. 2 (1998): 197–210.
83   Frow, "Elvis," 207.
84   Frow, "Elvis," 208.
85   Quoted in Doss, *Elvis*, 73.
86   Caldwell and Henry, "Living," 8.
87   Doss, *Elvis*, 112.

CHAPTER 2

1   *Friday Night with Jonathan Ross*, BBC 1, aired April 13, 2007.
2   Stuart Hall, ed., *Representation: Cultural Representations and Signifying Practices* (London: Sage, 1997), 2.

3	Hall, *Representation*, 2.
4	Hall, *Representation*, 61.
5	Hall, *Representation*, 3.
6	Jamie Merrill, "Bruce Springsteen and the E Street Band, Hyde Park, London," *Independent*, July 1, 2009, http://www.independent.co.uk/arts-entertainment/music/reviews/bruce-springsteen--the-e-street-band-hyde-park-london-1725854.html.
7	Hall, *Representation*, 4.
8	Hall, *Representation*, 4.
9	Hall, *Representation*, 21.
10	Hall, *Representation*, 5.
11	Quoted in Backstreets.com: Springsteen News, http://www.backstreets.com/news.html, accessed March 10, 2010.
12	Helen Davis, *Understanding Stuart Hall* (London: Sage, 2004), 180.
13	Stuart Hall, "Introduction: Who Needs Identity?" in *Questions of Cultural Identity*, ed. Stuart Hall and Paul du Gay (London: Sage, 1996), 2.
14	Hall, "Introduction," 6.
15	Hall, "Introduction," 6.
16	Hall, "Introduction," 13.
17	Cashmore, *Celebrity*, 43–50.
18	Cashmore, *Celebrity*, 43.
19	Boorstin quoted in Turner, *Understanding*, 5.
20	Boorstin quoted in Turner, *Understanding*, 5.
21	Boorstin quoted in Cashmore, *Celebrity*, 53.
22	Rojek, *Celebrity*, 10.
23	Rojek, *Celebrity*, 12.
24	Rojek, *Celebrity*, 10.
25	Rojek, *Celebrity*, 10.
26	Rojek, *Celebrity*, 10.
27	Rojek, *Celebrity*, 11.
28	Shallon Lester, "Newser Auditions to be Paris Hilton's 'BFF,'" *New York Daily News*, April 14, 2008, http://www.nydailynews.com/gossip/2008/04/15/2008-04-15_newser_auditions_to_be_paris_hiltons_bff.html.
29	Lester, "Newser."
30	"Paris Hilton Biography," Biography.com, http://www.biography.com/articles/Paris-Hilton-11271420 (accessed November 17, 2009).
31	"Paris," Biography.com.
32	"Paris," Biography.com.

33 Rojek, *Celebrity*, 17.
34 Rojek, *Celebrity*, 17.
35 Rojek, *Celebrity*, 18.
36 Rojek, *Celebrity*, 18.
37 Rojek, *Celebrity*, 20–21.
38 Rojek, *Celebrity*, 21.
39 Cashmore, *Celebrity*, 203.
40 Cashmore, *Celebrity*, 203.
41 Cashmore, *Celebrity*, 205.
42 Quoted in Gamson, *Claims*, 66.
43 Mark Frith, *The Celeb Diaries* (London: Ebury Press, 2008), 41.
44 Frith, *Celeb*, 41.
45 Gamson, *Claims*, 38.
46 Gamson, *Claims*, 38.
47 Cashmore, *Celebrity*, 19.
48 Cashmore, *Celebrity*, 20.
49 Cashmore, *Celebrity*, 20.
50 Frith, *Celeb*.
51 Frith, *Celeb*, 45.
52 Gamson, *Claims*, 65.
53 Gamson, *Claims*, 65.
54 Gamson, *Claims*, 66.
55 Gamson, *Claims*, 80.
56 Gamson, *Claims*, 80.
57 Gamson, *Claims*, 94.
58 Nina Sahu, "Paris Hilton Remains Oz Girls' Top Celeb Role Model," TopNews.in, October 14, 2008, http://www.topnews.in/light/paris-hilton-remains-oz-girls-top-celeb-role-model-217954.
59 Richard Dyer, *Heavenly Bodies: Film Stars and Society* (London: Routledge, 1986), 7.
60 Dyer, *Heavenly*, 7.
61 Dyer, *Heavenly*, 7.
62 Dyer, *Heavenly*, 15.
63 Dyer, *Heavenly*, 16.
64 Dyer, *Heavenly*, 16.
65 Dyer quoted in Cashmore, *Celebrity*, 193.
66 David P. Marshall, ed., *The Celebrity Culture Reader* (London: Routledge, 2006), 6.
67 Marshall, *Celebrity*, 12.
68 Marshall, *Celebrity*, 12.

69   Marshall, *Celebrity*, 6.

70   Cashmore, *Celebrity* 13.

71   Cashmore, *Celebrity*, 13.

72   Cashmore, *Celebrity*, 13.

73   Michael Basil Quoted in Cashmore, *Celebrity*, 175.

74   David Lewis and Darren Bridger quoted in Cashmore, *Celebrity*, 175.

75   Cashmore, *Celebrity*, 183.

76   Cashmore, *Celebrity*, 183.

77   Cashmore, *Celebrity*, 183.

78   P. David Marshall quoted in Cashmore, *Celebrity*, 263.

79   Morin, *Stars*, 78.

80   Virginia Blum quoted in Cashmore, *Celebrity*, 111.

81   Frow, "Elvis," 2007.

82   Twitchell, *Adcult*, 38.

83   Twitchell, *Adcult*, 39.

84   Stuart M. Hoover, *Religion in the Media Age* (London: Routledge, 2006), 9.

85   Wade Clark Roof, *Spiritual Marketplace: Baby Boomers and the Remaking of American Religion* (Princeton: Princeton University Press, 1999), 68–69.

86   Roof, *Spiritual*, 69.

87   Roof, *Spiritual*, 70.

88   Roof, *Spiritual*, 71.

CHAPTER 3

1   Gordon Lynch, ed., *Between Sacred and Profane: Researching Religion and Popular Culture* (London: I. B. Tauris, 2007), 126.

2   Daniel A. Stout and Judith M. Buddenbaum, "Approaches to the Study of Media and Religion: Notes from the Editors of *The Journals of Media and Religion* with Recommendations for Further Research," *Religion* 38 (2008): 230.

3   Stout and Buddenbaum, "Approaches," 230.

4   Tylor quoted in Brian Morris, *Anthropological Studies of Religion: An Introductory Text* (Cambridge: Cambridge University Press, 1987), 101.

5   Catherine Bell, *Ritual: Perspectives and Dimensions* (Oxford: Oxford University Press, 1997), 4.

6   Morris, *Anthropological*, 101.

7   Bell, *Ritual*, 4.
8   Herbert Spencer quoted in Morris, *Anthropological*, 97.
9   See Lynch, *Between*.
10   George Bernard Shaw quoted in Morin, *Stars*, 1.
11   Eric Michael Mazur and Kate McCarthy, eds., *God in the Details: American Religion in Popular Culture* (London: Routledge, 2001), 17.
12   Mazur and McCarthy, *God*, 13.
13   William Robertson Smith quoted in Bell, *Ritual*, 4.
14   Quoted in Bell, *Ritual*, 5.
15   J. G. Frazer, *The Golden Bough: A Study in Magic and Religion* (London: Macmillan, 1922).
16   Bell, *Ritual*, 5.
17   Frazer, *Golden*, 507.
18   Frazer, *Golden*, 507.
19   Rojek, *Celebrity*, 78–86.
20   Rojek, *Celebrity*, 79.
21   Emile Durkheim, *The Elementary Forms of Religious Life* (New York: Free Press, 1995), 22–26. First published 1912.
22   Emile Durkheim quoted in Bell, *Ritual*, 24.
23   Bell, *Ritual*, 24.
24   Durkheim, *Elementary*, 44.
25   Durkheim, *Elementary*, 44.
26   Roger O'Toole, *Religion: Classic Sociological Approaches* (Toronto: McGraw-Hill, 1984), 79.
27   Durkheim quoted in O'Toole, *Religion*, 79.
28   Durkheim, *Elementary*, 44.
29   Bell, *Ritual*, 24.
30   Durkheim, *Elementary*, 208.
31   Durkheim, *Elementary*, 208.
32   Bell, *Ritual*, 66.
33   Clifford Geertz, *The Interpretation of Cultures* (New York: Basic Books, 1973), 90.
34   Bell, *Ritual*, 66.
35   Clifford Geertz quoted in Bell, *Ritual*, 66.
36   Bell, *Ritual*, 67.
37   Mazur and McCarthy, *God*, 6.
38   Frow, "Elvis," 201.
39   Frow, "Elvis," 202.
40   Frow, "Elvis," 203.

41   Rudolf Otto, *The Idea of the Holy*, 2nd ed. (Oxford: Oxford University Press, 1950), 8.
42   Otto, *Idea*, 10.
43   Otto, *Idea*, 10.
44   Otto, *Idea*, 10.
45   Otto, *Idea*, 11.
46   Otto, *Idea*, 12.
47   Otto, *Idea*, 15.
48   Otto, *Idea*, 17.
49   Mircea Eliade, *The Sacred and the Profane: The Nature of Religion* (New York: Harvest Books, 1959), 10.
50   Eliade, *Sacred*, 11.
51   Eliade, *Sacred*, 11.
52   Eliade, *Sacred*, 20.
53   Eliade, *Sacred*, 21.
54   Eliade, *Sacred*, 21.
55   Eliade, *Sacred*, 12.
56   Eliade, *Sacred*, 12.
57   Eliade, *Sacred*, 12.
58   Eliade, *Sacred*, 13.
59   Eliade, *Sacred*, 204.
60   Eliade, *Sacred*, 205.
61   Eliade, *Sacred*, 206.
62   Lynch, *Between*, 136.
63   Lynch, *Between*, 136.
64   Lynch, *Between*, 138.
65   Paul Heelas, ed., *Religion, Modernity, and Postmodernity* (Oxford: Blackwell, 1998), 3.
66   Heelas, *Religion*, 3.
67   Heelas, *Religion*, 4.
68   Heelas, *Religion*, 5.
69   Heelas, *Religion*, 5.
70   Heelas, *Religion*, 9.
71   Heelas and Woodhead, *Spiritual*, 2.
72   Heelas and Woodhead, *Spiritual*, 2.
73   Heelas and Woodhead, *Spiritual*, 3.
74   Heelas and Woodhead, *Spiritual*, 3.
75   Roof, *Spiritual*, 66.
76   Roof, *Spiritual*, 66.
77   Roof, *Spiritual*, 66.

78   Roof, *Spiritual*, 67.
79   Roof, *Spiritual*, 67.
80   Roof, *Spiritual*, 69.
81   Roof, *Spiritual*, 69.
82   Roof, *Spiritual*, 69.
83   Stout and Buddenbaum, "Approaches," 227.
84   Stout and Buddenbaum, "Approaches," 228.
85   Hoover, *Religion*, 9.
86   Roof, *Spiritual*, 70.
87   Roof, *Spiritual*, 70.
88   Roof, *Spiritual*, 71.
89   Roof, *Spiritual*, 71.
90   Roof, *Spiritual*, 72.
91   Mazur and McCarthy, *God*, 10.
92   Mazur and McCarthy, *God*, 2.
93   Mazur and McCarthy, *God*, 3.
94   Ken Burns quoted in David Chidester, *Authentic Fakes: Religion and American Popular Culture* (Berkeley: University of California Press, 2005), 36.
95   Chidester, *Authentic*, 40.
96   Chidester, *Authentic*, 40.
97   Chidester, *Authentic*, 43–48.
98   Chidester, *Authentic*, 50.
99   Chidester, *Authentic*, 15.
100   J. Seguy quoted in Danièle Hervieu-Léger, *Religion as a Chain of Memory* (New Brunswick, N.J.: Rutgers University Press, 2000), 67.
101   Hervieu-Léger, *Religion*, 76.
102   Hervieu-Léger, *Religion*, 81.
103   Hervieu-Léger, *Religion*, 104.
104   Hervieu-Léger, *Religion*, 104.
105   Meredith McGuire, *Lived Religion: Faith and Practice in Everyday Life* (Oxford: Oxford University Press, 2008), 5.
106   McGuire, *Lived*, 5.
107   Robert Orsi quoted in McGuire, *Lived*, 13.
108   McGuire, *Lived*, 13.
109   Doss, *Elvis*, 73.
110   Doss, *Elvis*, 74–75.
111   Doss, *Elvis*, 76.
112   Doss, *Elvis*, 76.
113   John D. Caputo, *On Religion* (London: Routledge, 2001), 89.

114   Caputo, *On Religion*, 90.
115   Caputo, *On Religion*, 90.
116   Caputo, *On Religion*, 90.
117   Caputo, *On Religion*, 111.
118   Caputo, *On Religion*, 111.
119   Caputo, *On Religion*, 111.
120   Tom Beaudoin, *Virtual Faith: The Irreverent Spirituality of Generation* X (San Francisco: Jossey-Bass, 1998), 42–45.
121   Beaudoin, *Virtual*, 41.
122   Beaudoin, *Virtual*, 41.
123   Beaudoin, *Virtual*, 60.
124   Beaudoin, *Virtual*, 75.
125   Beaudoin, *Virtual*, 81.
126   Beaudoin, *Virtual*, 94.
127   Beaudoin, *Virtual* 110–11.
128   Marcel Cobussen, *Thresholds: Rethinking Spirituality through Music* (Aldershot: Ashgate, 2008), 146.
129   Cobussen, *Thresholds*, 146.
130   Cobussen, *Thresholds*, 148.
131   Cobussen, *Thresholds*, 148.
132   Cobussen, *Thresholds*, 149.
133   Eliade, *Sacred*, 205.
134   Hervieu-Léger, *Religion*, 67.
135   Lynch, *Between*, 138.
136   Geertz, *Interpretation*, 90.
137   Mazur and McCarthy, *God*, 6.

Chapter 4

1   John Calvin, *Institutes of the Christian Religion*, I, 11.
2   Reasonable Robinson, "Tiger Woods Fallen Angel or Willy Loman," Gullibility Blog, December 12, 2009, http://gullibility.blogspot.com /2009/12/tiger-woods-fallen-angel-or-willy-loman.html.
3   "These Are Your Gods Now: Forbes AnnouncesIts Celebrity 100," Defamer.com, June 12, 2008, http://defamer.gawker.com/5016015/ these-are-your-gods-now-forbes-announces-its-celebrity-100.
4   Matthew Miller, Dorothy Pomerantz, and Lacey Rose, eds., "Celebrity 100: The World's Most Powerful Celebrities," Forbes .com, June 3, 2009, http://www.forbes.com/2009/06/03/forbes-100 -celebrity-09-jolie-oprah-madonna-intro.html.
5   "These Are Your Gods," Defamer.com.

6   "Angelina Jolie's Friends Call Her 'Saint Angie'!" ShowbizSpy.com, February 17, 2010, http://www.showbizspy.com/article/200037/angelina-jolies-friends-call-her-saint-angie.html.

7   Alison Hill, "American Idols—The New Religion of Celebrity Worship," Associated Content, March 28, 2007, http://www.associatedcontent.com/article/189121/american_idols_the_new_religion_of.html.

8   John De Vito and Frank Tropea, *The Immortal Marilyn: The Depiction of an Icon* (Lanham, Md.: Scarecrow Press, 2006).

9   De Vito and Tropea, *Immortal*.

10   Gary Laderman quoted in Cathy Lynn Grossman, "Why Do We Have Celebrity 'Gods' Like Michael Jackson?" *USA Today*, June 26, 2009, Faith & Reason section, http://content.usatoday.com/communities/religion/post/2009/06/68492944/1.

11   Alan Smithee, "Do Celebrities Worship Themselves?" The African American Environmentalist Association Hollywood Blog, January 16, 2010, http://aaea-la.blogspot.com/2010/01/do-celebrities-worship-themselves.html.

12   Robert Graves, *The Greek Myths* (London: Penguin Books, 1955), 287.

13   Sam Vaknin, "Frequently Asked Questions #19," Samvak.tripod.com, The Narcissist's Addiction to Fame and Celebrity, http://samvak.tripod.com/faq19.html.

14   Vaknin, "Frequently," n.p.

15   Thomas Hobbes quoted in Leo Braudy in Marshall, *Celebrity*, 35.

16   Braudy in Marshall, *Celebrity*, 35.

17   Braudy in Marshall, *Celebrity*, 38.

18   Braudy in Marshall, *Celebrity*, 51.

19   Braudy in Marshall, *Celebrity*, 52.

20   Max Weber quoted in Alberoni in Marshall, *Celebrity*, 110.

21   Francesco Alberoni in Marshall, *Celebrity*, 110.

22   Alberoni in Marshall, *Celebrity*, 121.

23   Alberoni in Marshall, *Celebrity*, 122.

24   Richard Dyer quoted in John Langer in Marshall, *Celebrity*, 184.

25   Langer in Marshall, *Celebrity*, 184.

26   Langer in Marshall, *Celebrity*, 184.

27   Edgar Morin quoted in Langer in Marshall, *Celebrity*, 185.

28   Morin, *Stars*, 88.

29   Andrew Brown, "Jade Goody and the Diana Effect," *The Church Times*, April 9, 2009, 46.

30   Brown, "Jade Goody," 46.

31   Brown, "Jade Goody," 46.

32   Brown, "Jade Goody," 46.

33   Eliade, *Sacred*, 205.

34   Morin, *Stars*, 85.

35   Morin, *Stars*, 85–87.

36   Jill Neimark quoted in Cashmore, *Celebrity*, 251.

37   Deena Weinstein and Michael Weinstein, "Celebrity Worship as Weak Religion," *Word and World* 23, no. 3 (2003): 294.

38   Weinstein and Weinstein, "Weak," 298.

39   Weinstein and Weinstein, "Weak," 298.

40   Weinstein and Weinstein, "Weak," 300.

41   Weinstein and Weinstein, "Weak," 300.

42   Eamon Duffy, *The Stripping of the Altars: Traditional Religion in England. 1400–1580* (New Haven: Yale University Press, 1992), 160.

43   Duffy, *Stripping*, 161.

44   Duffy, *Stripping*, 161.

45   Leo Braudy quoted in Carlin Flora, "Seeing by Starlight: Celebrity Obsession," *Psychology Today*, July 1, 2004, http://www.psychologytoday.com/articles/200407/seeing-starlight-celebrity-obsession.

46   Helen Fisher quoted in Flora, "Seeing."

47   Flora, "Seeing."

48   Gary Laderman, "Celebrity Gods: The Religion of Stardom," Religion Link, January 4, 2010, http://www.religionlink.com/tip_100105.php.

49   Cashmore, *Celebrity*, 268.

50   Cashmore, *Celebrity*, 268.

51   Cashmore, *Celebrity*, 268.

52   Graves, *Myths*, 55.

53   Cynthia Cotts quoted in Cashmore, *Celebrity*, 144.

54   Richards, Wilson, and Woodhead, *Diana*, 1.

55   Richards, Wilson, and Woodhead, *Diana*, 1.

56   Richards, Wilson, and Woodhead, *Diana*, 2.

57   Richards, Wilson, and Woodhead, *Diana*, 3.

58   Richards, Wilson, and Woodhead, *Diana*, 4.

59   Julie Burchill quoted in Brunt in Richards, Wilson, and Woodhead, *Diana*, 24.

60   Hoover, *Religion*, 9.

61   See Graves, *Myths*, 371–77 and 462–65.

62   Diana Simmonds quoted in Brunt in Richards, Wilson, and Woodhead, *Diana*, 24.
63   Simmonds quoted in Brunt in Richards, Wilson, and Woodhead, *Diana*, 25.
64   Rosalind Brunt in Richards, Wilson, and Woodhead, *Diana*, 30.
65   Cashmore, *Celebrity*, 5.
66   Cashmore, *Celebrity*, 6.
67   Cashmore, *Celebrity*, 27.
68   Lapham quoted in Cashmore, *Celebrity*, 27.
69   Lapham quoted in Cashmore, *Celebrity*, 27.
70   Quoted in Morin, *Stars*, 85.
71   Morin, *Stars*, 85.
72   Morin, *Stars*, 84.
73   Morin, *Stars*, 84.
74   Alberoni, "The Piccolomini" (Act ii, Scene 4), quoted in Cashmore, *Celebrity*, 217.
75   Samuel Taylor Coleridge quoted in Thomas Bulfinch, *Myths of Greece and Rome* (London: Penguin Books, 1979), 11.
76   Cashmore, *Celebrity*, 5.
77   Cashmore, *Celebrity*, 5.
78   Cashmore, *Celebrity*, 5.
79   Gamson, *Claims*, 49.
80   Su Holmes in Anita Biressi and Heather Nunn, *The Tabloid Culture Reader* (Toronto: McGraw-Hill, 2008), 166.
81   Holmes in Biressi and Nunn, *Tabloid*, 166.
82   Holmes in Biressi and Nunn, *Tabloid*, 166.
83   Holmes in Biressi and Nunn, *Tabloid*, 166.

CHAPTER 5

1   Shane Watson, "What Kate Did," *Sunday Times Style Magazine*, January 24, 2010, 5.
2   Watson, "What Kate Did," 5.
3   Watson, "What Kate Did," 5.
4   Camille Paglia, *Sex, Art, and American Culture: Essays* (New York: Vintage, 1992), 14–18.
5   Paglia, *Sex*, 16.
6   Paglia, *Sex*, 16.
7   Paglia, *Sex*, 18.
8   Charlotte Martin, "Julia Right to Bare Her Mum Tum?" *The Sun*, May

8, 2009, http://www.thesun.co.uk/sol/homepage/woman/parenting/
      article2417285.ece#ixzz0dnXKzSwQ.

9   Martin, "Julia."

10   Martin, "Julia."

11   J. Hermes quoted in Turner, *Understanding*, 116.

12   Turner, *Understanding*, 116.

13   Hermes in Turner, *Understanding*, 116.

14   Hermes in Turner *Understanding*, 116.

15   N. Gabler quoted in Turner, *Understanding*, 116.

16   I. Connell quoted in Turner, *Understanding*, 117.

17   *Hello!* Number 1051, December 16, 2008.

18   John Walsh, "*Hello!* Magazine Celebrates its 20th Birthday,"
      Independent, May 9, 2008, http://www.independent.co.uk/news/
      media/hello-magazine-celebrates-its-20th-birthday-824252.html.

19   Borkowski quoted in Walsh, "Hello!"

20   Walsh, "Hello!"

21   Walsh, "Hello!"

22   *National Enquirer* September 15, 2008, 2–7.

23   "Jennifer Aniston—Biography," TalkTalk, http://www.talktalk
      .co.uk/entertainment/film/biography/artist/jennifer-aniston/
      biography/48?page=6 (accessed January 24, 2010).

24   *Hello!* Number 1051, December 16, 2008, 38.

25   *Hello!* 38.

26   *Hello!* 40.

27   Jolie quoted in Emine Saner, "Madonna and Child," *Guardian*,
      October 6, 2006, Family & Relationships section, http://
      lifeandhealth.guardian.co.uk/family/story/0,,1888924,00.html.

28   "Biography," The Official Josephine Baker Web site, http://www
      .cmgww.com/stars/baker/about/biography.html (accessed January
      24, 2010).

29   Turner, *Understanding*, 60.

30   Kylie Minogue quoted in Turner, *Understanding*, 52.

31   Braudy quoted in Turner, *Understanding*, 60.

32   N. Couldry quoted in Turner, *Understanding*, 61.

33   "Die Young, Stay Pretty," written by Deborah Harry and Chris
      Stein, copyright Monster Island Music.

34   "In Touch with Will Smith," *In Touch*, September 8, 2008, 69.

35   "In Touch with Will Smith."

36   "In Touch with Will Smith."

37   "In Touch with Will Smith."

38   *Hello!* June 24, 2008.
39   *Hello!* June 24, 2008.
40   Sharon Osbourne Official Site, http://www.sharonosbourne.com/ (accessed January 25, 2010).
41   "Beach Bodies," *Star,* September 8, 2008, 61.
42   R. De Cordova quoted in Turner, *Understanding,* 104.
43   "Nicole Richie Back in Shape Three Weeks after Giving Birth," HollywoodBackwash.com, September 28, 2009, http://www .hollywoodbackwash.com/nicole-richie-back-in-shape-three -weeks-after-giving-birth/ (emphasis in original).
44   Tom Leonard, "Tiger Woods Apologises for 'Transgressions' amid New Affair Claims," *Daily Telegraph,* December 2, 2009, http://www.telegraph.co.uk/sport/golf/tigerwoods/6711003/Tiger -Woods-apologises-for-transgressions-amid-new-affair-claims .html.
45   Tiger Woods, "Tiger Comments on Current Events," TigerWoods. com, December 2, 2009, http://web.tigerwoods.com/news/ article/200912027740572/news/.
46   Turner, *Understanding,* 105.
47   Turner, *Understanding,* 105.
48   John Hiscock, "Hugh Grant on Prostitutes Charge," *Daily Telegraph,* June 28, 1995, http://www.telegraph.co.uk/news/1471976/Hugh -Grant-on-prostitute-charge.html.
49   Quoted by Stephen M. Silverman in "George Michael Explains '98 Arrest," *People,* March 19, 2002, http://www.people.com/people/ article/0,,623803,00.html.
50   William Langley, "Indecent Exposure of Britney Spears' Meltdown," *Daily Telegraph,* January 6, 2008, http://www.telegraph .co.uk/news/worldnews/1574735/Indecent-exposure-of-Britney -Spears-meltdown.html.
51   Carole Lettieri quoted in Langley, "Indecent."
52   Langley, "Indecent."
53   Rojek, *Celebrity,* 80.
54   Rojek, *Celebrity,* 74–78.
55   Stephen Moyes, "Exclusive: Cocaine Kate," *Daily Mirror,* September 15, 2009, http://www.mirror.co.uk/news/top-stories/2005/09/15/ exclusive-cocaine-kate-115875-16133522/.
56   "Kate Moss Leaves US Rehab Clinic," BBC News, October 27, 2005, http://news.bbc.co.uk/1/hi/uk/4383244.stm.
57   Cashmore, *Celebrity,* 161.

58   Cashmore, *Celebrity*, 160.
59   "Elton John–Robbie Williams: Sir Elton John Forced Me into Rehab," Contactmusic.com, August 30, 2004, http://www.contactmusic.com/new/xmlfeed.nsf/story/robbie-williams.-.sir-elton-john-forced-me-into-rehab.
60   "Elton John," Contactmusic.com.
61   Cashmore, *Celebrity*, 218.
62   Cashmore, *Celebrity*, 218.
63   Cashmore, *Celebrity*, 219.
64   Cashmore, *Celebrity*, 219.
65   Cashmore, *Celebrity*, 220.
66   Cashmore, *Celebrity*, 222.
67   Frances Bonner quoted in Cashmore, *Celebrity*, 222.
68   Jessica Evans in Cashmore, *Celebrity*, 222.
69   Falana Fray, "Why Jamaica Should Make Bob Marley a National Hero," Itzcarribean.com, http://www.itzcaribbean.com/bobmarley4nationalhero.
70   Fray, "Why."
71   Roger Steffens, "About Bob Marley," PBS American Masters, http://www.pbs.org/wnet/americanmasters/episodes/bob-marley/about-bob-marley/656/.
72   Marcia Nelson, *The Gospel According to Oprah* (Louisville: Westminster John Knox, 2005), viii.
73   Nelson, *Gospel*, viii.
74   Nelson, *Gospel*, viii.
75   Phylis Tickle quoted in Nelson, *Gospel*, ix.
76   Nelson, *Gospel*, xii.
77   Jamie Phelps quoted in Nelson, *Gospel*, xiv.
78   Nelson, *Gospel*, xv.
79   Wade Clark Roof quoted in Nelson, *Gospel*, xii.
80   Nelson, *Gospel*, xiii.
81   Nelson, *Gospel*, xiii.
82   Nelson, *Gospel*, xviii.
83   Thomas Hauser, "The Living Flame," *Observer*, November 2, 2003, Observer Sport Monthly, http://observer.guardian.co.uk/osm/story/0,,1072751,00.html.
84   Hauser, "Living."
85   "Cruise Scientology Video Leaked," BBC News, January 16, 2008, http://news.bbc.co.uk/1/hi/7191355.stm.
86   Heelas and Woodhead, *Spiritual*, 2.

BIBLIOGRAPHY

"Actor Heath Ledger Dies at 28." CNN.com/entertainment, January 22, 2008. http://edition.cnn.com/2008/SHOWBIZ/Movies/01/22/heath.ledger.dead/index.html (accessed October 9, 2009).

"Angelina Jolie's Friends Call Her 'Saint Angie'!" ShowbizSpy.com, February 17, 2010. http://www.showbizspy.com/article/200037/angelina-jolies-friends-call-her-saint-angie.html (accessed February 18, 2010).

Barthes, Roland. *Mythologies*. Translated by Annette Lavers. London: Paladin Books, 1972. First published 1957.

Beaudoin, Tom. *Virtual Faith: The Irreverent Spirituality of Generation X*. San Francisco: Jossey-Bass, 1998.

Bell, Catherine. *Ritual: Perspectives and Dimensions*. Oxford: Oxford University Press, 1997.

Biressi, Anita, and Heather Nunn. *The Tabloid Culture Reader*. Toronto: McGraw-Hill, 2008.

Boyd, Malcolm. *Christ and Celebrity Gods*. Greenwich, Conn.: Seabury Press, 1958.

Bradley, Ian. *You've Got to Have a Dream: The Message of the Musical*. London: SCM Press, 2004.

Brook, Tom. "The Night Lennon Died." BBC News, December 8, 2000. http://news.bbc.co.uk/1/hi/entertainment/1060306.stm.

Brown, Andrew. "Jade Goody and the Diana Effect." *The Church Times.* April 9, 2009.

Bulfinch, Thomas. *Myths of Greece and Rome.* London: Penguin Books, 1979.

Caldwell, Marylouise, and Paul Henry. "Living Dolls: How Affinity Groups Sustain Celebrity Worship." Presented at the 2009 Association for Consumer Research (ACR) Asia-Pacific Conference, Hyderabad, India, January 4, 2009. http://neumann.hec.ca/aimac2005/PDF_Text/CaldwellM_HenryP.pdf.

Calvin, John. *Institutes of the Christian Religion.*

Caputo, John D. *On Religion.* London: Routledge, 2001.

Cashmore, Ellis. *Celebrity/Culture.* Abingdon: Routledge, 2006.

Chidester, David. *Authentic Fakes: Religion and American Popular Culture.* Berkeley: University of California Press, 2005.

Clark, Lynn Schofield. *From Angels to Aliens: Teenagers, the Media, and the Supernatural.* Oxford: Oxford University Press, 2003.

Cobussen, Marcel. *Thresholds: Rethinking Spirituality through Music.* Aldershot: Ashgate, 2008.

Crislip, Kathleen. "Tokens on Jim Morrison's Grave, Pere Lachaise Cemetery."About.com,2006.http://studenttravel.about.com/od/eftoursphotos/ig/Pere-Lachaise-Paris-Cemetery/morris_plach_ef_06.htm (accessed March 4, 2010).

"Cruise Scientology Video Leaked." BBC News, January 16, 2008. http://news.bbc.co.uk/1/hi/7191355.stm (accessed January 25, 2010).

Davis, Helen. *Understanding Stuart Hall.* London: Sage, 2004.

De Vito, John, and Frank Tropea. *The Immortal Marilyn: The Depiction of an Icon.* Lanham, Md.: Scarecrow Press, 2006.

Doss, Erika. *Elvis Culture: Fans, Faith, and Image.* Lawrence: University Press of Kansas, 1999.

Duffy, Eamon. *The Stripping of the Altars: Traditional Religion in England 1400–1580.* New Haven: Yale University Press, 1992.

Durkheim, Emile. *The Elementary Forms of Religious Life.* New York: Free Press, 1995. First published 1912.

Dyer, Richard. *Heavenly Bodies: Film Stars and Society.* London: Routledge, 1986.

Eliade, Mircea. *The Sacred and the Profane: The Nature of Religion.* New York: Harvest Books, 1959.

"Elton John–Robbie Williams: Sir Elton John Forced Me into Rehab."
    Contactmusic.com, August 30, 2004. http://www.contactmusic.
    com/new/xmlfeed.nsf/story/robbie-williams.-.sir-elton-john-forced
    -me-into-rehab (accessed January 25, 2010).

Fiske, John. "Opening the Hallway: Some Remarks on the Fertility of
    Stuart Hall's Contribution to Critical Theory." In *Stuart Hall: Critical
    Dialogues in Cultural Studies*, edited by David Morley and Kuan-Hsing
    Chen, 213–14. New York: Routledge, 1996.

Flora, Carlin. "Seeing by Starlight: Celebrity Obsession." *Psychology Today*,
    July 1, 2004. http://www.psychologytoday.com/articles/200407/seeing
    -starlight-celebrity-obsession (accessed February 18, 2010).

Fray, Falana. "Why Jamaica Should Make Bob Marley a National Hero."
    Itzcarribean.com. http://www.itzcaribbean.com/bobmarley4national
    hero (accessed January 25, 2010).

Frazer, J. G. *The Golden Bough: A Study in Magic and Religion*. London:
    Macmillan, 1922.

Friday Night with Jonathan Ross. BBC 1, aired April 13, 2007.

Frith, Mark. *The Celeb Diaries*. London: Ebury Press, 2008.

Frow, John. "Is Elvis a God? Cult, Culture, Questions of Method." *Inter-
    national Journal of Cultural Studies* 1, no. 2 (1998): 197–210.

Gamson, Joshua. *Claims to Fame: Celebrity in Contemporary America*. Berke-
    ley: University of California Press, 1994.

Geertz, Clifford. *The Interpretation of Cultures*. New York: Basic Books, 1973.

Glover, Stephen. "Stephen Glover: This Celebration of Ordinariness
    by the Media Leaves Me Bemused." *Independent*, February 23,
    2009. http://www.independent.co.uk/news/media/opinion/stephen-
    glover/stephen-glover-this-celebration-of-ordinariness-by-the-media
    -leaves-me-bemused-1629289.html (accessed September 5, 2009).

Graves, Robert. *The Greek Myths*. London: Penguin Books, 1955.

Grossman, Cathy Lynn. "Why Do We Have Celebrity 'Gods' Like
    Michael Jackson?" *USA Today*, June 26, 2009, Faith & Reason sec-
    tion. http://content.usatoday.com/communities/religion/post/2009/06/
    68492944/1 (accessed February 18, 2010).

Guzman, Monica. "Cobain's Legacy Still Evolving 15 Years after Sui-
    cide." *Seattle Post-Intelligencer*, April 8, 2009. http://www.seattlepi
    .com/pop/404942_cobain08.html (accessed October 9, 2009).

Hall, Stuart. "Introduction: Who Needs Identity?" In *Questions of Cultural Identity*, edited by Stuart Hall and Paul du Gay. London: Sage, 1996.

———. "On Postmodernism and Articulation: An Interview with Stuart Hall." In *Stuart Hall: Critical Dialogues in Cultural Studies*, edited by David Morley and Kuan-Hsing Chen. New York: Routledge, 1996.

Hall, Stuart, ed. *Representation: Cultural Representations and Signifying Practices*. London: Sage, 1997.

Hall, Stuart, and Paul du Gay, eds. *Questions of Cultural Identity*. London: Sage, 1996.

Hauser, Thomas. "The Living Flame." *Observer*, November 2, 2003. Observer Sport Monthly. http://observer.guardian.co.uk/osm/story/0,,1072751,00.html (accessed January 25, 2010).

Heelas, Paul. "Diana's Self and the Quest Within." In *Diana: The Making of a Media Saint*, edited by Jeffrey Richards, Scott Wilson, and Linda Woodhead, 98–118. London: I. B. Tauris, 1999.

Heelas, Paul, ed. *Religion, Modernity, and Postmodernity*. Oxford: Blackwell, 1998.

Heelas, Paul, and Linda Woodhead. *The Spiritual Revolution: Why Religion Is Giving Way to Spirituality*. Oxford: Blackwell, 2005.

Hello! Number 1051. December 16, 2008.

Hello! June 24, 2008.

Hervieu-Léger, Danièle. *Religion as a Chain of Memory*. New Brunswick, N.J.: Rutgers University Press, 2000. Originally published as *La Religion pour Mémoire*. Paris: Éditions du Cerf, 1993.

Hill, Alison. "American Idols—The New Religion of Celebrity Worship." Associated Content, March 28, 2007. http://www.associatedcontent.com/article/189121/american_idols_the_new_religion_of.html (accessed February 18, 2010).

Hiscock, John. "Hugh Grant on Prostitute Charge." *Daily Telegraph*, June 28, 1995. http://www.telegraph.co.uk/news/1471976/Hugh-Grant-on-prostitute-charge.html (accessed January 22, 2010).

Hockaday, Mary. "Michael Jackson Coverage." BBC News, June 29, 2009. http://www.bbc.co.uk/blogs/theeditors/2009/06/michael_jackson_coverage.html (accessed September 29, 2009).

Hoover, Stuart M. *Religion in the Media Age*. London: Routledge, 2006.

Jeffries, Stuart. "Obituary: Jade Goody." *Guardian*, March 22, 2009. http://www.guardian.co.uk/media/2009/mar/22/jade-goody-obituary (accessed September 29, 2009).

Johnson, Robert K. *Reel Spirituality: Theology and Film in Dialogue*. Grand Rapids, Mich.: Baker Books, 2000.

"Kate Moss Leaves US Rehab Clinic." BBC News, October 27, 2005. http://news.bbc.co.uk/1/hi/uk/4383244.stm (accessed January 25, 2010).

Khan, Urmee. "BBC Criticised over Jade Goody Coverage." *Daily Telegraph*, March 25, 2009. http://www.telegraph.co.uk/news/newstopics/celebritynews/jade-goody/5045083/BBC-criticised-over-Jade-Goody-coverage.html (accessed September 29, 2009).

Laderman, Gary. *Sacred Matters: Celebrity Worship, Sexual Ecstasies, the Living Dead, and Other Signs of Religious Life in the United States*. New York: New Press, 2009.

———. "Celebrity Gods: The Religion of Stardom." Religion Link. January 4, 2010. http://www.religionlink.com/tip_100105.php (accessed February 18, 2010).

Langley, William. "Indecent Exposure of Britney Spears' Meltdown." *Daily Telegraph*, January 6, 2008. http://www.telegraph.co.uk/news/worldnews/1574735/Indecent-exposure-of-Britney-Spears-meltdown.html (accessed January 21, 2010).

Lawrence, Cooper. *The Cult of Celebrity: What Our Fascination with the Stars Reveals about Us*. Guilford, Conn.: Skirt, 2009.

Leonard, Tom. "Tiger Woods Apologises for 'Transgressions' Amid New Affair Claims." *Daily Telegraph*, December 2, 2009. http://www.telegraph.co.uk/sport/golf/tigerwoods/6711003/Tiger-Woods-apologises-for-transgressions-amid-new-affair-claims.html (accessed January 21, 2010).

Lester, Shallon. "Newser Auditions to be Paris Hilton's 'BFF.'" *New York Daily News*, April 14, 2008. http://www.nydailynews.com/gossip/2008/04/15/2008-04-15_newser_auditions_to_be_paris_hiltons_bff.html (accessed November 17, 2009).

Lynch, Gordon, ed. *Between Sacred and Profane: Researching Religion and Popular Culture*. London: I. B. Tauris, 2007.

Maltby, John, Liza Day, Lynn E. McCutcheon, Raphael Gillett, James Houran, and Diane D. Ashe. "Personality and Coping: A Context for Examining Celebrity Worship and Mental Health." *The British Journal of Psychology* 95 (2004): 411–28.

Maltby, John, David C. Giles, Louise Barber, and Lynn E. McCutcheon. "Intense-Personal Celebrity Worship and Body Image: Evidence of a Link Among Female Adolescents." *The British Journal of Health Psychology* 10 (2005): 17–32.

"Marc Bolan's Rock Shrine." The Shady Old Lady's Guide to London. http://www.shadyoldlady.com/location.php?loc=373.

Marshall, David P., ed. *The Celebrity Culture Reader*. London: Routledge, 2006.

Martin, Charlotte. "Julia Right to Bare Her Mum Tum?" *The Sun*, May 8, 2009. http://www.thesun.co.uk/sol/homepage/woman/parenting/article2417285.ece#ixzz0dnXKzSwQ (accessed January 25, 2010).

Mazur, Eric Michael, and Kate McCarthy, eds. *God in the Details: American Religion in Popular Culture*. London: Routledge, 2001.

McCutcheon, Lynn E., Rense Lange, and James Houran. "Conceptualization and Measurement of Celebrity Worship." *The British Journal of Psychology* 93 (2002): 67–87.

McGuire, Meredith B. *Lived Religion: Faith and Practice in Everyday Life*. Oxford: Oxford University Press, 2008.

Merck, Mandy, ed. *After Diana: Irreverent Elegies*. London: Verso, 1998.

Merrill, Jamie. "Bruce Springsteen and the E Street Band, Hyde Park, London." *Independent*, July 1, 2009. Music section. http://www.independent.co.uk/arts-entertainment/music/reviews/bruce-springsteen-the-e-street-band-hyde-park-london-1725854.html (accessed February 10, 2010).

Miller, Matthew, Dorothy Pomerantz, and Lacey Rose, eds. "Celebrity 100: The World's Most Powerful Celebrities." Forbes.com, June 3, 2009. http://www.forbes.com/2009/06/03/forbes-100-celebrity-0-jolie-oprah-madonna-intro.html (accessed February 19, 2010).

Mizruchi, Susan L. *Religion and Cultural Studies*. Princeton: Princeton University Press, 2001.

Morin, Edgar. *The Stars*. Translated by Richard Howard. Minneapolis: University of Minnesota Press, 2005. First published 1972.

Morley, David, and Kuan-Hsing Chen, eds. *Stuart Hall: Critical Dialogues in Cultural Studies*. London: Routledge, 1996.

Morris, Brian. *Anthropological Studies of Religion: An Introductory Text.* Cambridge: Cambridge University Press, 1987.

Moyes, Stephen. "Exclusive: Cocaine Kate." *Daily Mirror,* September 15, 2009. http://www.mirror.co.uk/news/top-stories/2005/09/15/exclusive -cocaine-kate-115875-16133522/ (accessed January 2, 2010).

Nelson, Marcia. *The Gospel According to Oprah.* Louisville: Westminster John Knox, 2005.

"Nicole Richie Back in Shape Three Weeks after Giving Birth." HollywoodBackwash.com, September 28, 2009. http://www .hollywoodbackwash.com/nicole-richie-back-in-shape-three-weeks -after-giving-birth/ (accessed January 22, 2010).

O'Toole, Roger. *Religion: Classic Sociological Approaches.* Toronto: McGraw-Hill, 1984.

Otto, Rudolf. *The Idea of the Holy.* 2nd ed. Oxford: Oxford University Press, 1950.

Paglia, Camille. *Sex, Art, and American Culture: Essays.* New York: Vintage, 1992.

———. *Vamps and Tramps: New Essays.* London: Penguin Books, 1994.

"Religious Nuts Worship Michael Jackson." CelebrityFIX, ninemsn. com. http://celebrities.ninemsn.com.au/?blogentryid=360412&show comments=true (accessed September 10, 2009).

Richards, Jeffrey, Scott Wilson, and Linda Woodhead, eds. *Diana: The Making of a Media Saint.* London: I. B. Tauris, 1999.

Riddle, R. B. "The Man Tupac Amaru Shakur Remembered." HELLOarticle.com. http://www.helloarticle.com/the-man-tupac-amaru -shakur-remembered-r3182.htm (accessed March 9, 2010).

Robinson, Bryan. "Why Are Michael Jackson's Fans So Devoted?" ABC News/Entertainment, February 23, 2005. http://abcnews .go.com/Entertainment/LegalCenter/Story?id=464753&page= 2Fans (accessed September 5, 2009).

Rojek, Chris. *Celebrity.* London: Reaktion Books, 2001.

Roof, Wade Clark. *Spiritual Marketplace: Baby Boomers and the Remaking of American Religion.* Princeton: Princeton University Press, 1999.

Sahu, Nina. "Paris Hilton Remains Oz Girls' Top Celeb Role Model." TopNews.in, October 14, 2008. http://www.topnews.in/light/paris -hilton-remains-oz-girls-top-celeb-role-model-217954 (accessed November 17, 2009).

Saner, Emine. "Madonna and Child." *Guardian*, October 6, 2006. Family
    & Relationships section. http://lifeandhealth.guardian.co.uk/family/
    story/0,,1888924,00.html (accessed January 24, 2010).

Shiels, Maggie. "Web Slows after Jackson's Death." BBC News, June
    26, 2009. http://news.bbc.co.uk/1/hi/8120324.stm (accessed Septem-
    ber 29, 2009).

Silverman, Stephen M. "George Michael Explains '98 Arrest." *People*,
    March 19, 2002. http://www.people.com/people/article/0,,623803,00
    .html (accessed January 22, 2010).

SLyvetteRob. Comment on "So Do We All Have Celebrity Worship
    Syndrome? Lol," The MJFC Michael Jackson Fan Club, comment
    posted September 2, 2009. http://www.mjfanclub.net/mjforum373/
    showthread.php?t=13261 (accessed September 5, 2009).

Smithee, Alan. "Do Celebrities Worship Themselves?" The African
    American Environmentalist Association Hollywood Blog, January
    16, 2010. http://aaea-la.blogspot.com/2010/01/do-celebrities-wor-
    ship-themselves.html (accessed February 18, 2010).

Steffens, Roger. "About Bob Marley." PBS American Masters. http://
    www.pbs.org/wnet/americanmasters/episodes/bob-marley/about
    -bob-marley/656/ (accessed January 25, 2010).

Stout, Daniel A., and Judith M. Buddenbaum. "Approaches to the
    Study of Media and Religion: Notes from the Editors of *The Journal
    of Media and Religion* with Recommendations for Further Research."
    Religion 38 (2008): 226–32.

"Suge Knight and Many More on 2Pac's Death." AllEyezonMe.com,
    September 20, 1996. http://www.alleyezonme.com/2pacinterviews/
    tupacshakur/16/Suge_Knight_Interview.html (accessed March 8,
    2010).

Sylvan, Robin. *Traces of the Spirit: The Religious Dimensions of Popular Music*.
    New York: New York University Press, 2002.

"These Are Your Gods Now: Forbes Announces Its Celebrity 100."
    Defamer.com, June 12, 2008. http://defamer.gawker.com/5016015/
    these-are-your-gods-now-forbes-announces-its-celebrity-100
    (accessed February 18, 2010).

Turner, Graeme. *Understanding Celebrity*. London: Sage, 2004.

Twitchell, James B. *Adcult USA: The Triumph of Advertising in American Culture.* New York: Columbia University Press, 1996.

Vaknin, Sam. "Frequently Asked Questions #19." Samvak.tripod.com, The Narcissist's Addiction to Fame and Celebrity. http://samvak.tripod.com/faq19.html (accessed February 18, 2010).

Walsh, John. "*Hello!* Magazine Celebrates Its 20th Birthday." *Independent,* May 9, 2008. http://www.independent.co.uk/news/media/hello-magazine-celebrates-its-20th-birthday-824252.html (accessed January 23, 2010).

Watson, Shane. "What Kate Did." *Sunday Times Style Magazine.* January 24, 2010.

Weinstein, Deena, and Michael Weinstein. "Celebrity Worship as Weak Religion." *Word and World* 23, no. 3 (2003), 294–302.

Williamson, Judith. "A Glimpse of the Void." In *After Diana: Irreverent Elegies,* edited by Mandy Merck, 25–28. London: Verso, 1998.

Winston, Diane, ed. *Small Screen, Big Picture: Television and Lived Religion.* Waco, Tex.: Baylor University Press, 2009.

Woods, Tiger. "Tiger Comments on Current Events." TigerWoods.com, December 2, 2009. http://web.tigerwoods.com/news/article/200912027740572/news/ (accessed January 21, 2010).

INDEX